L Meriton

Money Masters All Things

L Meriton

Money Masters All Things

ISBN/EAN: 9783744796354

Printed in Europe, USA, Canada, Australia, Japan

Cover: Foto ©Suzi / pixelio.de

More available books at **www.hansebooks.com**

MONEY
Masters all things.

The scope and summe of what this Book doth say
Is, Pecuniæ obediunt omnia.

1. *On the Longevity of Moneys Regency.*

THough Madam Money, look both briske and gay
    Lovely and fresh as Blooming Flowers in *May*;
    Yet she for several Centuries of years
    Has Reign'd, as it by Sacred Writ appears.
For *Ephron Zohars Son,* for Moneys sake
Assurance unto *Abraham* did make,
Of *Machpelah,* and th' Cave within that space,
That he might have it for a Burying place:
Abraham possession took thereof and made
Room in the Cave, and *Sarah* therein laid;
Three thousand and five hundred years are past,
Since this, and more, yet money walks as fast,
And vigorously, as if but in her prime,
And never had been known before our time:
Yet she in former times hath born great sway,
Judas for her, his Master did betray :
Since which near seventeen hundred years are spun,
And yet she strenuously about doth run :

For Madam *Pecunia* will ne'er be Old,
So long as Sun and Moon their course do hold,
As she in former Ages did Enchant
And men lead as she pleas'd, she still does vaunt,
That she's grand Mistress yet of the same Art,
And doth not cease we see to Act her part,
Her Company to gain, men wait and Tend,
And her they'l seek and Court, to the Worlds end.

2. *On the Restraint and prohibition of* Money's *free passage.*

WHen Royall power, or states, do put Restraint
On Money's passage, folks make great complaint
City nor Country know not how to Live,
If they to Money freedom do not give :
When she's prohibited by the Command
Of supreme power, to pass from Hand to Hand,
Both Rich and Poor do sadly then complaine,
For without her, all Comfortless remaine :
The Gripeing Usurer must now forbear,
Cause Money is compell'd to disappear,
No debts can now be got, tho long time due,
Till she peeps out again, 'tis vain to sue,
Land-Lords must want their Rents, at their Rent day,
Money's proscrib'd so Tennants can not pay :
Tradesmen are heartless, live 'twixt hope and fear,
With carefull thoughts, now Money'l not appear,
Yeomen

Yeomen and Husbandmen do ſtay at home
With longing minds, to hear when Money'l come,
Poor Labourers are ready now to weep,
They know not how their Families to keep;
If Moneys company they can not have,
They're then quite out of hopes their Lives to Save :
'Tis ſhe Revives the Gentleman and Clown,
Where ſhe comes not, all hearts are there caſt down;
When ſhe's at Liberty all Men are glad,
But when Reſtrain'd, they then are almoſt mad;
For her Reſtraint does all Mens minds perplex,
She's Salus Populi, Suprema Lex,
For when Men fret, and fume, are full of Gall,
If Money Interceeds, ſhe quiets all.

3. *On the power, of Money in general.*

MOney the Goddeſs, is which all Adore,
She charmes the Vniverſe with her bright Ore,
All ages, ſexes, and Opinions be,
Greatly in Love with this ſame deitie,
Her Votaries, ſhe hath in every ſtate,
And princes court, and other potentate,
In all caballs, and Meetings ne'er ſo cloſe,
She by her Charmes, their Secrets can diſcloſe,
Cunning hatcht plots thought to be ſurely laid,
Have been by her diſcover'd, and Betray'd;
And ſhe by her Infatuating power,
Hath ſhew'd the company, the place and hour;

The

The greateſt Secrets and moſt private things,
Acted by Popes, or Emperors, or Kings,
For love of Money have been plainly ſhown,
Which otherwiſe would never have been known :
In Country, Camp, and Court, ſhe beares the Sway,
And is ſo prevalent, ſhe's ne'er ſaid Nay :
Her power can raiſe to Honour, or throw down
A Noble-Man, and raiſe a ſilly Clown ;
If you deſire to have your Princes ear,
Make uſe of her, and then you need not fear,
For ſhe into the preſence-Chamber brings
Some, that without her, ne'er ſhould ſpeak to Kings :
And makes the way to bring ſome into Grace,
Who neither merit Honour, nor a place,
Favour ſhe can procure at any time,
And make a dunce unto preferment Climbe,
When parts and worth Neglected are and ſit
Diſcouraged, and no Employment get :
Where ſhe does not appear to Interceed,
There is ſmall hopes your buſineſs will Succeed :
'Tis Money that procures a Man reſpect,
And want thereof, is Slighted with Neglect,

4. On the prevalencie of Money, at Elections for Members of Parliament.

IF you deſirous are, and have intent
To be a Member of the Parliament,

Where

Where choise of such is order'd to be made,
Make Money there your friend, and that's the Trade,
Befree but of your purse, Treat very high,
So Neighbours to the place, you may put by,
And Gentlemen of good Account you may
Our Vote, and by that means obtain the day :
Money will make the Burrough-Men all keen
To g.ve their Votes, though they have never seen
Your face, till the Election came in hand,
Yet now their tongues, and hearts you may command,
Money does many silly Men prefer,
To places of great Trust, when others far
More worthy for their parts, are set aside,
For Money in this Case, is the main guide;
And beares the Chiefest Rule in ev'ry place,
Men to preferment brings, favour, and Grace :

5. On *Moneys* Rule in the *Vniversities* and *Jnns* of Court.

IF you be at the Vniversity,
And there a very dunce, or Rakehell be,
Yet Batchelour, and Master too of Arts,
For Money you'l be made, tho you want parts,
And if you'd still advance to be more famous
Doctor you may proceed, then by Mandamus,
Without your keeping Acts or Exercise,
So whether you are Learn'd, or otherwise

Does

Does not appear, Money does falve up all,
She can a fool unto preferment call;
She can a Bifhop make and Confecrate,
And him Inftall, with Splendor and great ftate.
The meaneft Lawyer likewife we may fee
By Moneys help, oft call'd to the degree
Of Sergeant at Law, tho he've never Read;
And in's profeffion, is a dunder head:
Money has power, to raife him higher ftill,
For fhe a Judge can make him if fhe will.

6. On Divines.

MOney the grave divine makes to difpence
With all the Checks of Tender Confcience;
Swallow down any Oath, and never ftick.
Rather then lofe a fair Rich Bifhopprick,
Good Deanry, prebend, or fat perfonage,
They'l hazard all upon the publick Stage,
Of Cenfure, and Reproach, rather then fail,
If what they wifh to get, they may prevail,
Such are the Charmes of Money, that they will
Prove all things Lawfull by their Cunning Skill,
To their Advancement tends and eafie Lives,
And make their Children great, and Rich their Wives.

7. On Domeficke Chaplains.

IF you Domeftick Chaplain chance to be
Unto fome perfons of good Qualitie,

When

When ere my Ladies Woman fears she'l prove,
With Kidd unto her Master, he doth move,
The honest Chaplain some Respect to show,
Adviseth him the *Abigall* to woo,
Tells him her Lady such great care doth take
For her, that she will her a fortune make ;
And I too for my spouse sake, will bestow,
First Living that falls in my Guift on you,
That you with Comfort long may live together,
Solaceing your selves, in one another,
The hopes of cash, and Living too, do charm,
The Chaplain so, that he in Love grows warm,
He Courts the prostitute, who does seem Nice,
His Amours not Admitting in a Trice,
Yet after some Addresses she is won,
And so the Chaplain gets a Butter'd Bun,
Upon th' Enjoyment, he perceives a Cheat
On him is put, the Cushion some have beat
Before he came, and made it fit for use,
He's grieved in his mind at this Abuse,
But then bethinks himself since 'tis his Lot,
He must be pleased, whether he will or not,
And so his hopes do solely rest in this,
That now she's wed, she'l do no more Amiss,
And thus the Idol Money hath such power,
A man for Love of her, will wed a Whore,
He that wedds such, in hopes she'l honest prove,
May afterwards Repent his fond hot Love.

On

8. *On Non-Conformiſts.*

SOme-Non Conforms, we oft ſee Tempted are
To wear a Surplice, keep ſet forms of prayer,
Kneel at the Sacrament, great Reverence ſhow
To'th Altar, at the name of Jeſus Bowe,
And at the other Rites no ſcruple make,
And all this for a good Rich Living's ſake,
Which ſtore of Money doth them yearly bring,
For Love of whieh, they'd yield the Maſs to ſing:
This Goddeſs Reforms, and Transforms a Man,
Prevails with ſome, more then the Goſpell can.

9. *On the Quakers.*

THo ſome that ſeem hot *Quakers* will not Swear,
Yet when things of Advantage do appear,
By which great Proffit they may get, O then
They'l Lye, diſſemble, Cheat, like other Men,
The Light within them, by the Spirit fed,
For Love of Money is Extinguiſhed,
And the Old Man within 'em now bears ſway,
And ſo we're not to truſt their Yea and Nay,
Altho it be the *Quakers* Zealous Faſhion,
It is meer Cant, and great Diſſimulation.

10. *On perſons in high Imployments.*

MOney is ſure a Witch, and doth delude
Men in great place, aſwell as th' Multitude;

If fhe her glittering Spells before men caft,
They're Captivated, then and held fo faft,
Neither then, Wifdom, honour, honefty,
Nor place of greateft truft, nor Gravity
Can them Secure from this unhappy Fate,
Witnefs fome famous Men, but now of late,
Such is the force of Money at all times
That fhe can Aggravate or leften Crimes,
The Guiltlefs fhe can Guilty make we fee,
And can prevaile to fet the Guilty free.

11. On Judges.

MOney fhe can a Judges Eyes fo Blind,
That he the Truth can neither fee nor find ;
But is miflead into fome Error great,
Miftakes the Caufe ; I dare not fay a Cheat :
But he's fo ftrangely lead into miftake,
That he the greateft wrong for Right doth make ;
Mifreprefents the Evidence i'th' Caufe,
So th' Jury give, a Verdict, 'gainft the Laws.

12. On Juftices of the Peace.

TOth' Juftices of peace, men rarely bring
Money for favour, but fome other thing,
As Turkyes, Piggs, Geefe, Capons, they prefent,
To them, or to their Ladies with confent,
Or elfe the Clarks, by the poor Men are feed,
That th' Juftice may, at Seffions interceed,

And

And speak for th' Man, to get him a discharge,
Of his Recognizance, to go at large :
So tho to Money th' Justice is not bent,
Yet he will something take equivalent.

13. *On Lawyers.*

BOS in Lingua, hath been a Proverb long,
For Money truly charmes the Lawyers Tongue,
She stupifies his Sense and makes him Dumb,
He nothing sayes in's Clients Cause but mum,
Book cases he forgets, and of his sense
He's now depriv'd, has lost his Eloquence,
And Gingling harangues which the Lawyers use
The Cause to puzle, and court to Amuse ;
His wrangling Logick too, he us'd to have,
And urge in Court, his Clients Cause to save,
Is all now quite forgot, he cannot give
One single Reason now, th' Cause to retrieve.

14. *On Attorneys.*

MOney Attorneys, and Sollicitors too, Charmes,
To throw their Clients cause into her Armes;
Then th' business they neglect, and take no care,
Councel to fee or Witness to prepare,
Th' Client a Bailiff Fees, to Cry about,
Runs here and there, to find's Attorney out,
Who purposely Absconds, keeps out of sight,
And ne'er intends to do his Client Right ;

The

The Client, when too late, does underftand
His honeft Caufe was loft, 'caufe not well Man'd ;
He blames th' Attorney, who for his Excufe,
Begins his honeft Client to abufe,
Tels him, when as the Caufe in Court was nam'd,
'T appear in fuch a Caufe he was Afham'd,
And fays if he the truth had underftood
At firft, of's Clients Caufe not being good,
He'd not have meddl'd in't, So with a Scoff,
And a meer fham he puts his Client off,
Thus Money can Non-Suit, defaults can call,
Judgments Arreft, Money is all in all,
She can demur, o'erthrow or fave a Caufe,
On either fide, with or againft the Laws.

15. *On the Spiritual-Court Men.*

IF in the Spiritual-Court you chance to be
Prefented there, by fome for Baftardy,
Clandeftine Marriage, or fuch like offence,
The Court for ftore of Money will difpence
With any Crime, And for your Moneys fake,
You fhall difcharged be, no Penance make ;
But if this Idol's wanting, and you're poor,
You then are Sentenc'd by the Chancellour
Some Corporal penance publickly to make,
That others may by you Example take,
But in the other Cafe the Chancellour,
The Advocates, Proctors, and Regifter,

Whea

When each of them have got a good round Fee,
Then they contrive a way to fet you free,
If you Whoremonger be, or Whore, or Gilt,
Money prevailes to fet you free from Guilt.

16. On the Influence of Money in all Courts.

IN every Court, Experience fhews each day,
That Money, there doth bear great Rule and Sway.
In Chancery, or th' Kings-Bench, if fhe appear,
Or th' Court of Common-pleas, they her Revere,
Or inth' *Exchequer*, or at the *Affize*,
Or Seffions of the peace, fhe does Surprize;
For fho in every Office Regent fits,
And there at all times hath her luckie hits,
All Officers to her Obeyfance owe,
And do, when fhe appears, great Reverence fhow.

17. On Clerks of the Crown, and of the Peace.

CLerks of the Crown and peace, to bring about
Their Covetous defignes, oft Iffue out
Illegal procefs, Money by't to get,
And tho the people at fuch practice fret,
And Judge or Juftices, hear of the fame,
They'l find Excufes, to Evade the blame,
So its in vain to Clamour at the Wrong,
You may as well fit ftill, and hold your Tongue.
When Bailiffs come you muft pay what they ask,
Or they'l diftrain, tho its an heavy Task,

Money

Money to pay, where none is due of right,
But this we fee, is oft o'erfway'd with might,
Money and Friendfhip, does o'er mafter all,
Better fit ftill, than rife and get a fall.

18. On the Under-Sherriff, and affociate to the Clark of Affize.

FOR Money, the Subvic, keeps you at home,
So that you need not to th' *Affizes* come
And if you by Miftake, or in fome Hurry,
Happen to be Return'd on the grand-Jury,
If Money does appear, before the Eyes,
Of the Affociate to the Clark of th' 'Size,
He'l Skip your Second Call, no Bailiff Swears,
So you're difcharg'd from Service, and from fears,
May take your time and go now where you pleafe,
For you're at Freedom, and may take your Eafe.

19. On the Sherriffs Seal-Keeper.

THE Sherriffs Seal-Keeper, or Clark for Money,
Will give you fpeedy Notice when there's any
Mifchiefe againft you out, that you at home
May fave your felf, and Goods, before they come
To make a prey of you, and what you have.
So when the Bailiffs come, then they will Rave
And hunt about, and ftamp and tear like Mad,
When rot fo much as Fees, are to be had,

They

They being twice or thrice thus serv'd, you may
Compound, get easie payments to a day,
And by this means great Charges you may save,
Which Sheriff and the Bailiffs else would have.

20. On Bailiffs.

ALtho a Bailiff's chiefest Friend you are,
    Yet he for store of Coin, perhaps will dare
You to Arrest, or else he will betray
You to his Comrades, and shew how they may
Arrest you, tell the Time, and also where,
Which the poor harmless Man doth never fear,
'Cause his supposed Friend sits by demure,
So the poor Fellow thinks all is secure,
But at longrun, the Catchpoles hurry in,
And then the Judas rouzes, does begin
To fret and fume, and Quarrel every one,
When he himself in Truth's the cause alone;
And so behind Backs with a fleering Laughter,
The poor Man like a Sheep, is led to th' Slaughter;
By which we see a Rascal Bailiff will
His nearest and best Friend for Money sell.

21. On Goalers.

A Goaler will for Money kindness show,
    Irons keep off, above and not below
You're Lodg'd, may Eat and Drink too, at his Table,
Have any thing you lack, if you are able

To pay for it, but if you're poor you're thrown
In the Low Goal, no favour then is shown,
Altho your Case be pitiful and sad,
Yet there no Pitie, nor Regard is had,
But Money Friendship gets, does never fail,
Altho you're kept and Coopt up in a Goal.

22. On Witnesses in a Suite at Law.

MOney, makes Things so evident and clear,
To things before they're born, some men will swear
Then others she makes that they cann't Remember
Whether in *April* 'twas, or in *December*,
Or in what Year, or how the thing did happen,
He's now grown senseless, and has all forgotten,
Money distracts, takes memory quite away,
He knows not what was done but yesterday;
Memory she strengthens much, or doth decay,
Can make a Witness Swear just any way.

23. On Sea Officers.

THe Officers at Sea Money does Charm,
The Enemies may Sail by, without harm,
She Anchors them so fast, they cann't get free,
Or else the Fogs are thick they cannot see;
Until the Fleet of th' Enemy's past by,
And then the Officers do them discry,
O then they follow and pursue amain,
Discharge Broad-sides, but not a Man is Slain;

Or if there be, its fome unlucky fhot
The Mifchiefe doth, which they intended not.
Stores being gone, then they make of from Sea,
Get frefh Recruits Aboard, expect fome pay,
Then they to Sea again return to Cruife,
And fpend their Princes ftores in the like ufe
As they had done before, fo all this while
Their Prince of pay and ftores they do beguile,
Money where fhe attempts fhe doth prevail
Duty and Loyalty to fet to fale,
And Shipwrack makes of a good Confcience,
Makes breach of Truft and Oathes, feem no Offence,
Such power this Facinating Goddefs hath,
She makes men caft of Fear, and fhame, and Faith,
A Conquerefs we may her truly call,   ·
For Money does o'er Power, and Mafter all.

24. *On Privateers.*

THe Privateers do Cruife about the Main,
   Hazard their Lives and Ships, prizes to gain,
And then the Mafters muft Compound and pay,
Or elfe the Men and Ships, they Towe away,
But if it be thefe Roving Robbers Fate,
To fall i'th' Road of men of War, that wait
Thefe Privateers to Fight, and Seize upon,
And they are taken, then they're quite undone,
For th' men of War no Compofition take,
But thefe Men and their fhips, free prizes make,

                            Yet

Yet they in hopes of Money take their Lot,
And they themſelves ſome times do go to th' pot
Money's ſo prevalent, none can withſtand,
For her, Men venture, both by Sea and Land.

25. On Land Officers, in the Field or Garriſons.

IF Money to a General, does Appear,
She charges all, breaks through front, flanck and Rear,
This Dalilah enticeth, till at Length
She doth diſcover his whole Armies ſtrength,
Wherein it doth conſiſt, and how it lies ;
Then with her Luſture dazleth his Eyes:
He's taken with a Slumber, Senſeleſs made,
And no Alarum takes, till all's Betray'd,
His Army was ſo poſted that none could
Dream of Surprize, but oh the Power of Gold,
And Silver Charmes, Money's bright ſhining Twins;
O'Money, Money, when a War begins,
Thou canſt prolong it, or can make it ceaſe ;
Thy Umpirage determines War and Peace ;
Tho th' Cauſe be ne'er ſo juſt, when War's begun,
Yet without Money, it can not go on ;
'Tis ſhe procures both Armes, and Men to Fight;
She can defend the Wrong, o'erthrow the Right ;
Can make the Cannons to ſhut o'er or ſhort,
To batter, beat down, or not hurt a Fort,
Make Fuzees fire, or dye, and, Bombs fall down,
And to deſtroy or not deſtroy a Town :

Beſieger

Besiegers and Commanders Gold Bewitches,
Their Men cut of within their Mounds and ditches
Or wittingly Betray'd i'th' dead of Night,
And so Confusedly do make their flight,
Leaving their Guns, and Baggage for a prey
To the Besieged, when they run away.
As Money can Raise a Siege, before a Town,
So when before't an Army doth sit down,
And specious Termes unto the Town doth Tender,
She can entice them, Quickly to Surrender ;
Altho the place be strong, and can hold out,
Money can strangely bring the thing about,
Where Vigorous Assaults can not prevail,
Money can open th' Gates, and walls can Scale ;
Besiegers and Besieged, her obey ;
Its Money that does bear the Bell away ;
The Towns of greatest strength Money has won,
Which by the force of Armes could not be done;
Great *Lewis* knows't, this practice is his own,
For this, not force, hath gain'd him many a Town.
For Money, Officers false Musters make,
And also for this Tempting Idols sake,
Their Soldiers they will Cheat of Clothes and pay,
Quarters o'th' Tick leave, when they march away,
Money's so Tempting, when she comes to hand,
Rather than part, they'l hazard a disband,
She beares the Rule in great, aswell as small things.
For she we see, at all times Masters all things.

26. On Skippers, or Masters of ships.

MOney will make the Skipper Anchor weigh,
And in the foulest weather put to Sea,
And leave his Friends his Children and his Wife,
Hazard his Men, his ship too, and his Life,
So Charming is the glittering of this Ore,
That none can him perswade to stay on shore,
With or without a Wind to Sea he'l go,
Maugre his Friends, whether they will or no,
For Money is so much his hearts delight,
That neither stormes, nor Tempests him affright;

27. On Marchants.

MErchants no Ventures at the Sea would make,
Wer't not for hopes of gains and Moneys sake,
For if they thought that Money would not come,
Then they would keep their goods and ships at home,
'Tis Money makes them fearless of their loss,
Tho sometimes they come home by weeping Cross,
Yet they're not satisfi'd, but hope to find,
Fortune more favourable, and more kind,
So they'l Adventure still, and not give o'er
Their fresh pursuits, to gain this Guilded Ore,
Till some of them Adventure all they have
And so are brought, meer Bankrupts to their Grave,
Whilest others do Arrive to great Estate,
So Variable is all Humane Fate,

When

When Money's Courted, some times she will fly,
And of, herself, at other times draw nigh;
Tho she's a Witch as some have understood,
And doth a man oft 'times more harm than good,
Yet so delightfull all her Charmings are,
That poor and Rich in her desire a share;
So that in all things whether great or small,
We still do find that Money's all in all.

28. On Sea Men and Land Soldiers.

Give Sea Men Money and you may procure
These men the greatest Hardships to endure,
Despise all dangers Fight with might and main,
Money does make them fearless to be slain;
'Tis she makes Soldiers Fight, by Sea and Land,
Pay them but well, and then you may Command
And greater Numbers have in Readiness,
Then you have need for; without Drum or Press,
They would not hide themselves, run into holes,
But briskly throng to you, in numerous shoals;
The force of Money all things doth Command,
Navies at Sea, and Armies too by Land.

29. On the Custome Officers.

TOth' Custome waiters both by Land and Water,
How to get Money, is the only matter
At which they aim; for where they get a Fee,
Tho they be Sworn, yet they can oversee,

And

And hazard both, their Conſcience, and their place ;
For Moneys ſake, they'l venture a diſgrace ;
But when no Money does appear, O then,
They're in their Office very Zealous men :
Will make ſtrickt Search, and Rummage round about,
Diſcovery to make, and find things out,
For which there's duty or ſome Cuſtom due ;
Then they're ſevere, and will no Kindneſs ſhew,
But tell you that, they are upon their Oathes
And ſo will grope you round upon your Clothes,
That their be no Concealment by you made,
You muſt excuſe them, for it is their Trade :
Money the Eyes can cloſe, or open bring,
That they can ſee, or cannot ſee a thing ;
Things done in time or out of time all's one,
Or if not done at all, ſhe can Attone,
Make all things currant paſs at any time,
And can procure Excuſe for every Crime.

9. *On Sergeants at Armes, or purſevants.*

IF a Sergeant at Armes or Purſevant,
Be ſent for you, and Money you do want
To palm the Man, then he will ſearch about,
And make Enquiry till he find you out,
And then away he'l hail you in great haſt
He's other work in hand ſo can not waſt
His time to wait on you, but you muſt go
Along with him, whether you will or no,

B

But if you've ſtore of Money for a Fee,
And entertain him well, he'l overſee;
And ſo return again, leave you behind;
And make Return that you he could not find,
But when that he unto your Houſe did come
You'd taken a far Journey, gon from home;
The time you would return uncertain was,
So he was forc'd to let the buſineſs paſs;
Thus Money blinds his Eyes, he can paſs by,
And at's Return excuſe it with a Lye.

31. On Surveyors of Land.

IF there be Land that you would have Survey'd
And you th' ſurveyor would your friend have made;
Make Money then to him your ſureſt Friend,
She ſo effectually will recommend
You unto him, that you may him command
For to Return his Survey of the Land,
As you Inſtructions give, and do require,
He'l make it more or leſs as you deſire;
Money ſo tempting is that ſhe can have
A man for love of her become a Knave,
Rather than ſuffer Money to paſs by,
Men to oblige her, will both Swear and Lye.

32. On Stewards.

IF you would have a Farm at eaſie Rent,
Let my Lords Steward know, what's your intent,

Be

Be free to him, and he will bring't about
For he does always know when Farmes are out,
So if you ftore of Money to him bring,
At eafie Rent, he'l place you on the thing,
Will get you Licenfe fome frefh Land to plowe,
Or at fome Wood : and any kindnefs fhow ;
Th' Money proves a powerful advocate
In Country bufinefs and affairs of State.

33. *On Aftrologers or Nativity Cafters.*

AStrologers if you to them are free
Of Money, they'l caft your Nativity
To be Aufpitious, fortunate, long Life,
And if you be a Man, then a Rich Wife
You fure muft have, and if a Woman, fhe
Muft wed an Husband of great Quality,
Nought hut profperity fhall you attend,
When as your ftars do no fuch thing portend :
Money does make Men in their Judgements Err,
Juft as you pay them, fo they fhall declare,
If Nobly you do pay, good Fortune then,
If meanly, various 'tis, like other Men,
And in horary Queftions they do give
Good or bad Anfwers, as they do Receive,
More or lefs Cafh from you, out of your purfe,
So fhall their Anfwers be, better or worfe ;
Thus Money leads a Man which way fhe will,
Makes him forget his greateft art and skill :

And

To Right or wrong, he'l subscribe for her sake.

34. *On Officers of the Excise.*

TH' Exciseman, a Concealment will o'er look;
   For a good Fee, not Enter't in his Book
And where he has a kindness he will charge
At easie Rates, others set down at large,
For the Poor Ale-wives have in this no skil,
So th' Officers, may Charge them as they will
And whatsoe'er they set them down, they must
At the next siting pay, for there's no trust;
The general Riders, and Surveyors too,
This Idoll Money do adore and Woo,
Think nothing Troublesome, nor count it pain,
If they but this bright Goddess can obtain;
And likewise every other Officer,
Doth Complement, Cring, and make Leggs to her;
She can procure dispatch without delayes,
Or make you dance Attendance many daies,
For she can Expedite or can Foreslowe
Matters she can conceal, or Truth can show,
She any thing can do that you would have
She either can Condemn, or she can save.

35. *On Messingers.*

IF you are in Arrears of fee-Farm Rent,
   To th' King, a Messinger to you is sent;

And when he comes his fee you muſt firſt bring,
And pay to him, before you pay the King,
From th' Kings Exchequer, he tells you there's due
Eight pence a Mile, which he expects from you,
If Money you do want, he will diſtrain
So you muſt hunt about, for it's in vain
To think to put him off, for he will ſtay
And not ſtir from your Houſe, till he get Pay,
You time for th' Payment of the King may Crave,
But I, ſaith he, my Fee will ſurely have,
And when I come again, you may Expect
Each time I'le have my Fee, for your Neglect.
Himſelf and Horſe you kindly Entertain,
And you betimes i'th' Morning do complain,
No Money you can get, then he will take
A Silver Tankard, Cup, or Bowle, ſo make
Requital, in this baſe ungratefull way,
And then take Horſe, Farewell he can not ſtay;
And ſo the plate along with him muſt go,
He's the Kings Meſſinger, who dare ſay no,
The Love of Money doth moſt Men bereave
Of all that's good, no manners ſhe doth leave;
Conſcience, nor honeſty, where Men do ſet
Their minds on nought, but Money how to get.

36. *On Common Informers.*

COmmon Informers, oft times do pretend,
Men Guilty are, when they do not offend;

Tell

Tell them they have Tranfgreft, and broke the Law,
And fo they keep Poor filly Men in Awe,
Extorting Bribes by fraud and bafe deceit
For which fometimes, a pillory they get;
Then other whiles, where they do get a Fee,
They manifeft Offences will o'er fee,
So Money right or wrong, they'l furely have,
For fhe is the dear Solatrix they crave,
Moneys Memento, *remember* always in their Ear is,
Faciam ut mei Semper memineris,
The thoughts whereof do run fo in their mind,
Their all, they'l fet at ftake, Money to find,
Their Credit place, and Confcience fans Control,
For Money's fake, they'l pawn their precious Soul.

37. *On Church-Wardens, Surveyors of high ways, Overfeers of the Poor, Affeffors &c.*

CHurch-Wardens and Surveyors of th' high ways,
    Poors Overfeers, and Seffors, now a dayes,
And other Officers, altho they fwear,
Their Office truly to perform, they fear.
No Oath, nor do they ftand the leaft in awe
Either of Confcience, or of the Law,
If they can either Money get or fave,
Each of thefe Officers will be a Knave ;
Geting or faveing, is fuch a tempting thing,
They'l private perfons cheat, afwell as the King,

The

The Goddefs Money all Men Court and woo,
To compafs her they care not what they doo.

38. On Chief Conftables.

QUarterly Moneys on each Conftablery Charg'd,
Is fometimes by the Mafter chief Enlarg'd,
Six pence, a Groat, or three-pence in a Town,
Above the Sums, the Seffions does fet down,
Which Overplus he puts into his purfe,
Tho'tis a Cheat, he likes himfelf no worfe,
And tho he know, if it difcover'd be,
He fhall be punifht for fuch Knavery,
Turn'd out of place, Jndicted too, and Fin'd
Yet th' Love of Money runs fo in his mind,
He'l hazard both his Credit and good Name,
And wholly banifh fear of worldly fhame,
Such power's in Money, and fuch Feats fhe works,
That Chriftians, Heathens, and the Jews and Turks
And all perfwations fhe Charms to betray
Credit and Confcience too, her to obey.

39. On Confervators of Rivers.

COnfervators of Rivers, who are made
To look that Fifher-Men leave of their Trade,
In fpawning time, and when Fifh Kipper be,
If Money does Appear, they will o'er fee
And Noughty Fifh allow, not fit for ufe,
If Money pleads i'th' Fifher-Mens Excufe,

She

She can Excuse unlawfull Nets, and spears,
Lines, leisters, Trolls, Pots, Angles, Leaps, and weares,
And all unlawful Engines in the water,
If she but Wheedles up the Conservator,
He has no Power, her Charmes for to withstand,
If she intrust herself but in his hand,
O Charming Money with Bewitching wiles,
Men of their Honesty thou oft Beguiles.

40. On Post-Boyes.

MAny dark Night, and Cruel Stormy day,
In Frost and Snow, and filthy dirty way,
Poor post-Boyes ride, sometimes are drown'd or starv'd,
It's wonderfull how they shou'd be preserv'd :
This hardship they, Poor Creatures do endure,
Great hazards run, some Money to procure,
Money's the Darling solace of their mind,
And th' only chiefe Asilum of Mankind.

41. On Doctors.

WHen one is Sick, if Money do appear,
She can prevail to have the Doctor there,
And if she freely do attend the Man,
Then he'l prescribe the safest Rules he can,
And his Opinion tell of the Disease,
And will prescribe such things as shall give Ease,
Each time he comes, if he Receives a Fee,
Then frequently you shall the Doctor see,

And

And ſo long time as he does Money find,
He dayly ſhall add Comfort to your mind,
And ſay he hopes the danger is quite over,
When he's aſſur'd that you will not Recover ;
There's hopes of life, as long as he gets Chink,
But when that fails, he knowes not what to think,
He then looks ſleightly, and begins to ſay,
All hopes are paſt, you ſpend ſo faſt away,
He tells the ſick Mans Friends he can not Live,
He ſpeaks the Truth, when they've no more to give,
And if the Poor be ſick, he's then in haſt,
Or very buſie, hath no time to waſt,
Money muſt come herſelf, or elſe you muſt
Want his advice, for Docters will not Truſt ;
If he be ſure that he ſhall get no pay,
The Docter's Tongue-ty'd, he has nought to ſay ;
And ſo the Poor alone on God depend,
Whileſt th' Rich their Money on the Docters ſpend,
Which tho ſhe Maſters all things that have Breath,
She can not Lengthen life nor Maſter Death.

42. *Apothecaries.*

WHen the Apothecary gets a Bill
From th' Learned Docter, for ſuch Men as will
Good payment make, and where his Money's ſure,
For ſuch, he looks out drugs, both ſound and pure,
And in his Mortar them will ſtrongly beat,
And run his Peſtel round until he Sweat,

Then

Then make the phyſick truly up and Quick
And then the patient Viſit, that lies Sick,
At your Bed-ſide he takes hold of your Arm,
And in his Canting Termes, begins his Charm,
Does feel your pulſe, and ſayes he'l ſet you Right,
And talks, as if he'd Cure you upon ſight,
He to you then a Bottle ſmall doth bring,
And bids you taſt, Oh'tis a cordial thing,
Then he pulls out a pot of his Conſerve,
Which you muſt often take, it will preſerve
Your body Cool, repreſs exceſſive Thirſt,
But you muſt take of this ſame Bottle firſt
Sayes he, then many pots and Glaſſes more,
He leaves, t'inlarge his Bill, augment your ſcore,
Which ſignifie no more for you to Eat,
Than Chip in potage, for 'tis all a Cheat,
Then daily doth he, ſome ſlip ſlap or other,
Bring to your Chamber, and there doth them clother,
So thoſe that come to Viſit you, ne'er ſtop
To ſay, 'tis like th' Apothecaries Shop:
Money does make his Morter ſweetly Knell,
And if you've none, it Tolls your paſſing Bell,
Old Rotten drugs and Medicines he'l Try
For th' Poor, cares not whether they Live or Die,
For in ſuch caſe where Payment he doth fear
His Shop of Rotten Drugs, then he will clear;
If Money had the Power but life to give,
The Rich would never Die, Poor not Long live.

43. *On Romish Priests.*

IF you your Father Confeſſor do Feed,
With Caſh, you need not fear what life you lead,
For you may Kill, Rob, Steal, Drink, Whore, and Swear,
Inceſt Commit, without regard or Fear,
Or other ſins, for he can pardon all
Your great and Crying ſins, aſwell as ſmall :
And when you dye, if unto him you leave
A good round Summe, he then your Soul will ſave
From purgatory, It ſtraight to Heaven goes,
Evades all purgatory pains and Woes,
And ſo tho Money cann't prolong your days
Yet after Death, ſhe hath the power to raiſe
You unto Bliſs, if you have ſtedfaſt Faith,
For to Believe the Prieſt, In what he ſaith.

44. *On Clerks to Juſtices of the Peace.*

CLerks to the Juſtices of Peace, do Love
Money to get, they for her ſake will move,
And Vigorouſly for you will interceed,
If of your Purſe to them you freely Bleed,
And them fee Liberally, you then command
Their help for you, they Back and Edge with ſtand,
At Seſſions get diſcharge upon your call,
So that you need not there Appear at all,
Or any other Service they can doo,
Either at Seſſions, or at home for you,

Money

Money a Friend in Court, or other place
Can any time procure, she's in such Grace,
If Money comes, the Clark's your Friend ne'er fear it,
If she withdraw, Nullus Amicus erit.

45. On the Charms of Money in Horse Races, and Foot Courses.

IF you've a mind to keep a Running Horse,
A good Estate it craves, and a good Purse;
For when you match, tho you're assur'd to have
The Match, yet if the Rider prove a Knave,
He'l Money take, you falsly to Betray,
And will for want of Rideing lose the day,
Or throw your Horse, or out of Wind him Ride,
Or purposely, run on the Scoopes wrong side:
And so the Match and keeping too are lost,
Then home you come, and Fret to be so Crost.
In most Foot courses too, like Tricks are play'd,
When wagers are put down, Cheats then are made,
Such Charms and Power in Money are we know,
She makes the Horse or Foot, Run Swift or flow,
This Idol Money the whole world deludes,
Both private Persons, and whole Multitudes.

46. On Gripeing Land-Lords.

SOme Land-Lords minds on Money, are so Bent,
They never cease to Rack and Raise their Rent;
                                    Money

Money if they do but get, they do not matter
If the poor Tennants fit, with Bread and Water,
To Screwe and Squeefe the Men, they ne'er give o'er,
Until the Tennant's brought to Beggars door,
When they the days of payment can not keep
The Land-Lord's gone with all, then at a fweep,
And leaves the Poor Man and his Family
Unto the Charge and Care o'th' Conftablery,
Some men ne'er heed, if Money comes but in,
For they believe Oppreffion is no Sin.

47. *On Gamefters and Gaming.*

GAmefters at Cards will Cheat, and with falf Dice;
The Love of Money tempts them into Vice,
When taken with falfe play, they'l Damn and Swear,
To get their Prize will Stab Men without fear,
The deareft Friends will Quarrel to fuch height
When they're at Game, they'l one another Fight
The fordid humour, and Covetous defire
Men have for Money, does breed all this Ire,
Some fhe makes merry, and fome others Sad,
Some full of paffion, others ftaring Mad,
Such Strange Effects fhe woorks, as fhe thinks good,
Her Power's fo ftrong, fhe's not to be withftood.

48. *On Schoolmafters.*

THE pedigogue, who Rules as petty King,
Over his young Subiects; unto thofe who bring
In

In their Relief, and make him punctual pay,
Observing constantly their Quarter day,
O'er such, his Rule is gentle Mild and free,
But o'er the Rest 'tis perfect Tyranny
Money does make him kind, and pitifull
To Lads who are Jnsippient and dull,
He'l put them right, when they are at a Lofs;
To th' Boys that pay not well, he is more Crofs;
If they have not, Ad unguem every word,
Then he to them, no favour will afford,
But up they go forthwith at his Command,
And feel the Smart of his Correcting hand:
Dunces with Money, Friendship can obtain,
When wit without her, Friendlefs doth remain.

49. *On Petty Constables.*

THE Constable, that Ancient Officer,
The Idol Money some times doth prefer
Before his confcience, and for her fake,
The parties he will neither fee nor take
But make Return, that he can not them find,
Lets them Efcape, Money has made him Blind,
Tho he be fworn truly to Execute
His Office, th' Caufe is clear, needs no difpute,
Of Knavery to be Accus'd he's loth,
Yet Money, he prefers before his Oath,
And rather then this Charming Mifs he lack,
Credit and Confcience too, muft go to wrack.

5o

50. On Mountibancks.

THE Mountebanck he Traverfeth much ground,
To find the Place where Money doth abound,
Then up he fets his ftage, where every day
He fhews himfelf; Andrew the Fool i'th' play
For Money doth Appear, who for a wit,
Doth come behind his Mafter ne'er a Whit,
Thus Money can produce any difguife,
Can make a wife Man Fool, and Fool feem wife:
Then when from every Quarter of the Town
People are Crowded in to fee the Clown,
And gaz'd at him fome time, and Laught a while,
The Mafter then with Cring, and gracefull fmile,
Begins aloud, to fet forth and proclame
His own great Wondrous Merits and his Fame,
And tells what mighty Cures both far and near
He hath perform'd in each place here and there,
You may fays he, Enquire the Certainty ;
But you'd as good believe as go and fee,
After his long Harangue, he's very willing
To give you a fmall Packet for a fhilling,
Containing many Medicines, whofe worth
The little Printed paper doth fet forth,
But when you come ro Try thefe things indeed,
You'l find they're all but Cheats in time of need :
If you fhall wait with Money in your hand,
O then you may be certain to Command

His

Of Wen, Hair-Lip, or Cancer too he may
A Cure perhaps perform, and take away,
Which any Man can do, afwell as he,
That is but Skilfull in Chyrurgery ;
If you are Blind, or Deaf, and can not hear
He'l bid you truft to him, and do not fear,
For he will Cure and can Recover both,
But in fuch cafe to truft I fhould be loth,
For we can feldom hear or ever find,
That they the Deaf make hear, or Cure the Blind :
Money's the Tempting bait at which they Bite,
Care not if you ne'er hear, nor get your fight,
For that's the only thing, they hancker after,
If you ne'er mend, they turn't but to a Laughter.

51. *On Dancing Mafters.*

THE dancing Mafter will his Coopees fhow
His fteps, and Winds, if he of Money know
He'l skip about, and Nimbly dance and play,
When Entring pennyes come, or Quarter day,
Money makes both his heart and Feet fo Light,
That he can cut his Capers bolt upright,
But when he Money lacks he's fadly dull,
If not his Belly, yet his heart is full,
He's out of order then, ready to Swoond,
He fcarcely then can lift his Feet of ground,

Such

Such Vertue is in Money that 'fhe can
Put life and Spirit into any man,
When fhe appears to them ; but when fhe's gone,
Their hearts are dull, and heavy as a ftone.

52. On publick Waites.

THE publick waites who Liveryes do own,
And Badges of a City, or fome Town,
Who are retain'd in conftant Yearly pay,
Do at their Solemn publick Meetings play.
And up and down the Streets, and Town in cold
Dark Nights,when th'Jnftruments they can fcarce hold
They play about, and tell what hour it is,
And Weather too, this Courfe they do not mifs,
Moft part of Winter, in the Nights; and when
Some Generous Perfons come to Town, thefe Men
As foon as they're Inform'd, do then repair
Unto their Lodgings play them fome fine Ayre
Or brisk new tune, fuch as themfelves think fit,
And which they hope, with th' Gallants fancies hit,
They cry God Blefs you Sirs; again then play,
Expecting Money, e'er they go away,
For fhe's the Mifs that in their hearts doth Reign,
No waiting's fervile thought, this Mifs to gain,
All Trades, with all profeffions, and all Arts,
Money to compafs, do all Act their parts,
She makes a Jubile where e'er fhe ftayes,
And where fhe's not, they have but Anxious dayes.

U A   53. On

53. *On Fenceing Masters.*

THE Master of defence for Money will
   Appear upon the Stage, to shew his skill,
And Art in Fencing there, before Mens Eyes,
And publickly will Fight to get a prize,
Himself adventure to be Cut and Slasht,
And some times Main'd perchance, or soundly Gasht,
By his Antagonist, some times in Rage,
Disgracefully in scorn, thrown of the Stage;
So sprightly Vigorous is Moneys Charm,
He will Adventure both disgrace and harm,
Nay men about Miss Money make such stir,
That they will Resolutely dye for her.

54. *On the Bell Man.*

THE Bell Man at the Dead of Night walks round,
   And with an Hollow Voice, and dolefull sound,
Puts you in mind then of your later end.
Instructions gives, how you your Life should spend,
What time of Night it is, he doth declare;
Then to another place he doth Repair,
And thus from Night to Night, though ne'er so Cold,
In Frost and Snow, this Constant course doth hold,
And all this hardship he doth undertake
Without Complaint, for Madam Moneys sake
For he without her knows not how to Live,
So day and Night he will Attendance give,

And

And thinks no Service nor no pains too much,
For Moneys fake, his Love to her is fuch.

55. On High-Way-Men, and Padders.

SOme to get Money think no pains too great,
Others for Love of her, Lye Swear and Cheat,
But High-Way-Men and Padders for her fake,
Venture their all, and fet their Lives at ftake,
And whether they, by Horfe or Foot do Rob,
Perchance thofe they affault, may do their Job,
But if they're neither flain, nor foundly Bang'd,
Yet if they're taken, they'l be furely Hang'd,
And tho before hand, their hard Fate they know,
Yet they for Lady Moneys fake doe fhow,
Such Love and Kindnefs, that they value not
Her to obtain, if they're Kill'd on the fpot,
And few of them though long time they have paft,
But they are either kild, or hang'd at laft,
Money is fure a Witch, that can entice
Fond Men, to Run juft headlong into Vice,
And defperately to Act, and perpetrate
A Wickednefs, attended with fuch fate
Befides the Sin doth recompence their pains,
With Hanging, fometimes Gibbetted in chains.

56. On Vfurers.

IF you to borrow Money ftand in Need,
If your Security be good, you Speed,

But

But then the Vſurer he doth Expect
Payment of Jntereſt, you'l not Neglect,
Every ſix Moneths, or elſe beſure he'l call
Both for the Uſe, and for the Principal,
And if you're not provided to pay't in,
To threaten you with Law, he doth begin,
Then you muſt Treat th' Old Miſer, preſents make
To th' Wife, or Son, or Daughter, and them take
For Friends, that you may keep't to further day,
Till you the Summe are able to Repay ;
And thus they're harrazed, that Money lack
Enough to make their very Heart-ſtrings crack,
Money is ſure the Root of every Evil,
And th' Love thereof proceedeth from the Devil.

57. *On the Force and power of Money, in the preferment of Young Laſſes.*

THE Curious Girle come of good parentage,
   Of Comely body, Beautifull, right Age,
Endow'd with Natures prime and cheifeſt Arts ;
Which one would think, could charm beholders hearts,
Yet if ſhe Money lack, ſhe's only Gaz'd
And lookt upon, and for a Beauty prais'd,
But often ſtayes until her Beauty fade
Before ſhe's Courted, and a Wife is made,
And then the Courtſhip oft times proves to be
By thoſe who are below her Quality,

To whofe Embraces, fhe muft yield Confent,
Elfe fingle Life to lead, muft be Content.
Whereas the Squint-Ey'd, Lame, deformed Lafs,
If fhe have Money, doth for Beauty pafs,
Perfons of all degrees do her Admire,
Not for her Self; her Money they defire,
Which if fhe wanted, no Man would Endeavour
Her Love to gaine, But fhe might ftay for ever,
Curfe on this Money, that doth men Enfnare
To leave the fine, and take the Courfeft ware,
She forces Men deformities to woo
All Sizes, Ages, and all Colours too.

58. *On Clippers and Coyners.*

THE love of Money is fo prevalent,
   Some Men and Women are fo fully bent
In queft of it, that they will undertake
To fpoile the Currant Coin for lucre's fake
Clip, Round, or Wafh, Diminifh or Impair,
Or Falfifie, all which Offences are
Treafon by Law, and fuch as are difcry'd,
And guilty found thereof, when they are Tiy'd
Muft fuffer Death, with Scandal and difgrace,
On Sleds the Men are drawn unto the place
Where they their Ignominious Exit make,
And Womens Doom is Burning at a ftake.
Money fuch Perfons, furely does Enchant
Whofe minds and thoughts thefe Terrors do not daunt,

Her Charmes are wonderfull that can require
Men to be Hang'd, Women to Burn i'th' Fire.

59. *On Musitians.*

MUsitians run about from place to place,
To Wedings, Fairs, cock-fightings, and horse-race
And such like Meetings, hopeing there to find
Some frollick persons, to them will be kind,
And Money give them, which their hearts will Chear,
And please as well as musick doth the Ear,
No harmony like Money in one's Purse,
And where she's not, noe Sadnes can be worse,
Money's the universal Anodyne,
And of more Solace, than Musick or Wine
Where e'er she comes and stayes she makes men glad,
Dispels all grief, they need not then be Sad.

60. *On Sextons or Bell Ringers.*

THE Sexton every Morning and each Night,
Winter when Dark, and Somer when it's Light,
Enters the Church, though it be ne'er so Cold,
Maugre all phantasms there, with Courage Bold,
And then at th' noted hour, does Ring the Bell,
That all the Neighbours, round about may tell
How th' Night does pass away, and day draws on,
That so the People may then think upon,
What Business they have then, to go about;
And thus the Sexton the whole year throughout
Observes

Obferves his hour, and at the Quarter day
Do's call upon his Mafters for his pay :
'Tis Money that he works for, that's the thing,
That makes him time obferve, and Bell to Ring,
For if he had no Money to Receive,
He'd Ring no Bell, nor no Attendance give.

61. On the Common Cryer.

THe Common Cryer walks about, with's Bell,
At certain places makes his ftand, to tell
And publifh things, that he is to make known
To ftrangers, and to th' People of the Town,
This he performs, for mean and forry Fees,
Some Money's better far, then none he fees,
And of th' Old faying, he does notice take,
That many littles, does a Mickle make ;
For Money, Men are willing to take pains,
And rather then Idle fit, for little gains.

62. On Miners,

MIners that work below within the ground,
For Coals, Lead, Tinn, or Iron, oft are found
Crufh'd by the falling in of Earth to Death,
Or fulphurous damps do Rife, and ftop their Breath
The Love of Money makes them thus to venture
For therein does their Chiefeft comfort Center,
It's their Alexicacon, and no Evil
They fear, if Money comes, no not the Devil ;

Money

Money Poor Souls they do so highly prize,
To compass her all dangers they despise,
Into the Dark and deepest pits they'l Sink,
Midst noisome Vapours down, even to hell's brink,
Adventure Life, and Limbs, and all that's dear,
For Moneys sake, banish all panick fear;
Men boldly vndertake and fearless are
In things, where Money falls unto their share.

63. On Common Fowlers.

THe common Fowlers which do mak't their Trade,
In many Carr, and Plash of water wade,
In Hail, and Frost, and Snow, they go about,
Walk here and there, in hopes to find Game out,
And all this pains they take with willing Mind,
Because thereby they Money get, they find,
Which cheers their hearts, and Minds, when they her get,
Altho their hands, and feet, be cold and wet,
Let Poverty or Riches, be ones Fate,
Money's Consolabund in every State.

64. On the Arms Painters.

IF to th' Arms Painter, you do tell your Name,
He'l quickly find a Coat out for the same,
And he will tell you for a good round Fee,
That it belongs unto your Family,
When as perchance, if you fall into strife,
You have as good a Right to th' Heralds Wife;

Yet

Yet he for Money will fuch kindnefs fhew
He'l give you Coat, and Creaft, and Mantling too,
And all in Colours neatly will difplay,
Deliver't then to you, to take away,
Which you may ufe, and by it Cut a Seal
And Challeng't as your own, he'l not reveal,
Your Money ftops his mouth, he'l filent be,
Altho he knows 'tis Cheat and Fallacy;
He that has Money, may take anothers Right
And keep and ufe it, in the Owners fight,
Money makes wrong be Right, and Right be wrong,
She makes a Man to fpeak, or hold his Tongue,
She's the Enchanting pharmacentria
Whoes powerfull Charmes can lead Men any way.

65. On Moneys Efficacy, in gaining feeming Love to Old Men, and Old Women.

MOney will make a Frefh young Buckfom Lafs,
Let an old crazy Dotar'd her Embrace,
She'l think him brisk and frefh as Rofe in June,
If wanted wealth, fhe'd fing another Tune,
And him which now Enjoyes her Maiden-head,
She would difdain, and fly his hated Bed,
But fhe her brisk Amours does foon forfake,
And her Old man fhe doth a Cuckold make,
And that's the Fortune of Old Silly Fools,
That match themfelves to fuch young airy Tools.

The Withered Old Woman, if she've store
Of Cash, the young Gallant will her Adore,
And Swears she's Lovely, he dyes, if he miss her,
Whereas if Poor, she'd make him Spewe to Kiss her,
Th' Old Creature does believe, is at's Command,
Pleights him her Troth, and gives to him her hand,
Consents to Marriage, he visits her each day,
And she like a young Girl doth Toy and play,
At length the day doth come, that they are Wed,
And he against his stomach, goes to Bed,
He Kisses her, and sore against his will
Her old Lascivious humour doth fulfil :
Thus for a while, he'll please, and slights her not,
Till he her Money, Gold, and Bonds has got,
And then he weary grows, and can not Kiss,
Loathes her Embraces, must now keep a Miss,
Under her Nose, for th' pleasure of his life,
With whom he'l Kiss, in spight of his Old Wife,
Th' old Woman storms, that she's so much Neglected,
And th' gay Flurting Miss is so Respected,
She sighs and sobs, that she alone must lye
And her brisk Youth abhors her Company,
And nought delights him now, but his young Miss,
But such the Fruits of such a Marriage is,
For Youth and Age, are very seldom found
In their Embraces, constant firm and Sound,
The one Repents the Folly they're run in,
Whilest th' other wallows in their Lust and Sin,

Equality

Equality in Age, and in degree,
And Fortunes too, make the best Sympathy.

66. *On Farmers Husband-men and Grayfiers*

THE Farmer Husband-man, and Grayfier keep
   Their Cattel, Horses, Butter, Corn, and sheep,
And several Markets Try, both far, and near,
Having still hopes, to Sell their goods out dear;
Their Cattel they will Comb, and Horns will greafe,
That they may viewly look, and Chapmen please,
Their facks, and pokes, with well dreft Corn they'l face,
When that within's ill Dreft, and very bafe,
A Sample of their fineft Corn they'l get,
Seldom deliver th' reft, like unto it,
For that was done, to draw the Bargain on,
They care not, how th' Corn's dreft, when that is done,
Such Tricks as thefe they have, Money to gain,
And many more. For her they beat their Brain,
She is the only thing for which they Toyle,
Early and Late, and work, and Sweat, and Moyle,
And when they Money get, fhe brings Relief,
And Recompenfeth all their Care and Grief,
But when they Money want, they can not Reft,
For then with grief and care, they are oppreft.

67. *On Millers.*

WHen Corn is dear, the Miller often is
   (To get great gains) Tempted to do amifs,

'Not

Not pleas'd with's due, Exceffive Toll he'l take,
And all the Country Cheat, for Moneys fake,
But the Old Saying is, as hath been told,
An honeft Miller hath a Thumb of Gold.

68. On the Influence Money hath amongft Labourers and work-People.

IF you want work-men, and they are but fcant,
Pay well, and give good Wage, you need not want
Carpenters, Mafons, Slators, and Lime-Burners,
Brick-Layers, Tilers, Shinglers, Joyners, Turners,
Smiths, Plummers, Glafiers, Leaders of Sand,
Thatchers and Gardiners, you may command,
Or other Workmen; Money is their Blifs,
They think that there no greater Comfort is;
When Mowers, Rakers, and Reapers, are but few,
Two pence advance in Wage, procures enow,
When neither love nor favour can procure 'em,
Yet powerfull Money failes not to fecure 'em;
For where they get beft wage, and fureft pay,
Thofe Mafters they will follow and obey.

69. On Gardiners.

IF ftandards, or wall-Trees, you mean to plant,
And with a Gardener treat, for thofe you want,
No fort of fruit Trees, you can eafily name,
But he'l affure you, he has fome o'th' fame,

But

But his are of the Choicest Fruit, and best,
That can be had, so price above the rest
Of Common Gardeners, he'l have for his Trees,
And thus he wheedles you, at length agrees
To furnish you with some of every kind,
And so he Money gets to please his Mind;
And hats the thing which he hath in pursuit,
And you must take your hazard of the Fruit;
So er patience had for some few years,
And length, Crab, sower, and mean trash Fruit appears,
At which you're vext to find the fellows Cheat,
You send for him, can scarce forbear to beat
The Man, you call him Rascal Rogue and Knave,
He caps and Cringes, does your patience crave,
To hear him speak; he did not understand
Your soil so well as now; there's too much Sand,
Or Clay or Mud, or Gravel in your ground,
There lyes the Mischief Sir, I now have found,
And that's the reason why your Fruit proves nought,
For there's no fault I'm sure, i'th' Trees you bought,
I have some Trees right for this soil will prove,
Else you shall have them all Sir, For your Love,
Thus both your time and Money you have lost,
And by this Cheat, you're put to double cost,
Before he brings you Trees, he knowes are right,
Altho he cold have done it at first sight;
But Money was the thing the Man did covet,
All Sciences and Trades, do fondly Love it,

They

They care not what they do for Love of gain,
No Cheats nor Tricks for Money they'l refrain.

70. On the Provident Country House-wife.

THE frugal Wife, hath great care in her Head,
She Riseth early, and late goes to Bed,
She is more Thrifty in her house then any,
She'l nothing wast, she thinks will make a penny,
If ought be broke, or out of order set,
She Chides her Servants, and is in a Fret,
To mind her Chirn, Bowls, Dishes, and Milk-pale,
Be Scowr'd, and Washt, and Scalded, she'l not fail,
And all her Vessel kept, Neat, Sweet, and Clean,
No Sluttishness about her Milk is seen,
She minds to keep the same, both sweet and good,
And so she doth her Bread, and Drink, and Food,
In Brewing, Bakeing, and in dressing Meat,
She's frugal, cleanly, and Exceeding neat;
Enough's a Feast, so more she will not have,
Profuseness she's against, resolves to save,
For she's not given to a Lavish folly
Better have many Meals than few and Iolly,
Her Cream into the Chirn, she sees pour'd in
And minds her Maids be clean, when they begin
To Churn, and that they have no nasty Clout
About them then, nor lick nor take none out,
She makes them take't clear out, when th' Butter's got,
Then strains the Milk through sieve into a pot,

Thus

Thus she saves all, to th' bignefs of a Nut
And she that does not fo's, a Carelefs flut,
Then she doth wash it clean with water fair,
Leaves not a Moat therein, nor the least hair,
Then weighs it up, and for the Market makes it,
And there, all those that know her, quickly takes it;
To th' making then of Cheese, she takes great Care,
Minds that the Rennet's Sweet, and Cheese meat's fair,
In clean Cloths put, each time they go to th' prefs,
And there fet ftraight, not flubber'd in by guefs,
Her Curds when they're at height, she takes up all,
Leaft they unto the Kettle bottom fall,
Drowfie and Sleepy moft Maids are, she knows,
So she doth look to th' Milking of her Cows,
Their paps she'l have well drawn, they muft not leave,
So long as th' Cows a drop of Milk will give,
Her Hogs and Calves then, she will have well ferv'd,
If to her Maids she truft, they'l be half ftarv'd,
For th' Meat's fome times fo thin, and Cold they get,
That they'l not lye their Mouths to't, but take pet,
Then otherwhiles they make't fo hot indeed,
To death they'd fcald them, if she did not heed,
Her turkyes, Geefe, and Ducks she minds each day,
Makes them convenient Nefts, when they do lay,
And when their Nefts they Feather and would fit,
Such number of choice Eggs, she'l for them fit
As she thinks they can Cover well and Brood
When they come off, there's Water fet and food,

But then she minds, when from the Nests, they're rais'd,
They stay not too long off, least th' Eggs be daz'd,
The time of hatching, she knows very well,
And then observes, and helps to crack the shell,
If she perceives the young-ones are but weak,
She helps them then, out of the shell to break,
And carefull is to get them brought up fit,
For th' Market, or for her own Pot or Spit,
Her Hens to count each Night she will not fail
And with her Finger grope them in the —————,
And such as are with Egg, she doth secure,
No Eggs can then be lost, she is right sure;
Then when her Hens do sit, she Careful is
As for her other Fowl, there's nought amiss ;
She at the Winnowing of Corn will be,
To have't well drest, and no wast made she'l see,
If th' wind be high, to Winnow then she's loth,
Least any of the Corn blow of the Cloth,
When th' Corn is fit to measure, she takes care
To do't herself, or see't done, when she's there,
Into some Garner then, the Corn's convey'd,
For th' house use there or for the Market layd;
A good Wife thus, takes care in every thing,
Which she conceives or knows will Money bring,
Money's the Solace of her mind and heart,
To compass which noughts wanting on her part,
She toils all day, and in her Bed contrives
All ways for Money, few such carefull Wives,

Her

Her mind runs after that will Money bring,
And she will Money make of any thing,
The saying's old, but much Truth doth contain,
Unthrifty Wives waſt more than Husbands gaine,
For th' Husband that would thrive, and Riches have,
Muſt in ſuch caſe his Wifes permiſſion crave.

71. On the different Effects wrought by Money, between the Neceſſitous Perſon, and the Miſer.

MOney if we do but conſider't well,
We find produceth good Effects and ill,
She the Neceſſitated doth Relieve,
And out of Miſerie doth them Retrieve,
She brings them Comfort, when their hearts are down,
And makes them Courage take, 'gainſt fortunes frown,
But to the Miſer, ſhe's another thing,
Money great Miſchief unto him doth bring,
The more he gets, the greater is his Curſe,
For he thereby becomes ſtill worſe, and worſe,
The more he hath, he ſtill doth Covet more,
And will not ceaſe till Death calls at his door,
Then all his hourded Treaſure he would give,
To Bribe and put of Death, that he might Live,
But now he ſees the folly of his gains,
They cannot life prolong, nor eaſe his pains,
Money no Comfort now affords the Man,
When he begins to look pale faint and wan,

And sick to Death, O then, he doth Express
Great grief and Sorrow for his Wickedness,
And if he were to Live again, he would
Abhor the eager gripeing after Gold,
But death's inexorable and gives no dayes
No pleadings he admits of for Delayes,
But when he comes poor Mortals to Arrest,
They Natures debt must pay, without Contest.

72. On Moneyes Influence over some Girles, and Wives.

MAny fine Girl and Wife, through long pursuit
With Money tempted is to prostitute
Her Curious Body, and to pawn her honour
To some young Gallant, that is brisk upon her,
And thus this Idol Money doth entice
Many fine Creature to submit to Vice,
And great debauchery, without Control,
To th' hazard both of Body and of Soul.

73. On Moneyes strange Charmes in breeding Quarrells, or Reconsiling differences.

GReat is the power that is in Money had,
The force thereof produceth good and bad
This wicked Idol makes dear Friends fall out,
Great Foes to be great Friends, she brings about,

Money

Money can make Men one another fue,
And Act fuch things, which afterwards they'l rue,
Nay fhe can make them one another Fight,
And Murder out of hand fome times in fpight,
She Quarrels breeds, and alfo Reconfiles,
Which way fhe will, fhe leads Men with her wiles:
Nor wit, nor Force, is able to withftand,
Her Charmes are fuch, fhe all Men does Command.

74. *On the Power of Money amongft poor Labouring Men.*

IF you to let a piece of Work defire,
The Labourer, that duely works for hire,
Will take it, and will Labour very fore
To get two pence, or three pence fometimes, more
Than daily Labour comes to, fo the Man
Works late and early, with all ftrength he can,
And when he gets his Wage, it Chears his heart,
With Joy to's Wife and Children he'l depart.

75. *On Butter Buyers or Factors.*

THE Butter Buyers 'mongft themfelves agree,
How they may Gull, and Cheat the Country,
They know poor Farmers are enforcft to fell,
So they do make the price juft as they will,
Higher or lower, prices they fet down,
As they fee more or lefs come to the Town,

When

When there does come, plenty of Firkins in,
Then to th' Poor Men they stories do begin,
Tell them at London th' Markets are so low,
That how to buy and save, they do not know,
Tho not a word of this they know is true,
Yet by this Artifice, they Wrest and Screw
Great proffit to themselves, and Money get,
From th' honest Farmers, without much Regret:
These Buyers 'mongst themselves low prices make,
Which the Poor Farmers are enforcst to take,
For Money they do want, else had not come,
So sell they must, Money to carry home;
But when these Factors Orders do receive
To Buy a parcell quickly up, they'l give
Twelve-pence advance Perhaps, or some times more,
But when they're serv'd the price is as before,
And thus the County is brought to submit,
And take such prices, as these Men think fit;
If you a Pound or more, do want of weight,
Then you must make Abatement for it straight,
But if your Firkin proves a pound or two
O're weight, for that they nothing will allow,
At every Turn, proffit they're sure to make,
And all the Country Cheat, for Moneys sake.

76. On Corn Marchants, and Malsters.

COrn Marchants, and the Malsters chiefest Care,
Is Grain to buy cheap in, and sell out dear.

When

When Farmers, and poor Husband men, would fell,
Wages to pay, or Rents to Raife, they fmell
Their want of cafh ; then are they very fhy
Are full of Corn, want Money, can not buy,
But if they can but bring you to their Pin,
They'l Bargain then, your Corn you may bring in,
And thus does Run Poor Mens unhappy Fate,
They muft for Money fell at any Rate ;
But when the Buyers have got pritty ftore.
And for fome time refolve to buy no more,
Then they bethink themfelves whether laft Year,
Or this, they did their Corn buy in more dear
If the laft year, great ftore of Old they have,
If this more dear, they could no old ftore fave,
So all muft go at the beft price they give,
And by this means they're Rich, and bravely live,
If Money can but any wayes be had,
It's welcome tho the means be ne'er fo bad,
When as a fteeping failes, and th' malt's not Right,
Then that is mixt, layd in fome place in fight,
To fend abroad to thofe whofe Cuftome they
Do not Regard, becaufe they badly pay,
But thofe that take up much, and take great Care
To make good payment, get the choifeft ware,
So runs the world, thefe that have Money may
Have any thing, where'ts wanting, they're faid Nay.

77. *On Jobbers of Cattel.*

THE Jobber buying Cattel, doth contrive
    To some Remote farr market them to drive,
Where he's in hopes, they will good profit bring,
And that alone, is the desired thing,
At which he aimeth, and all People Covet,
For all mankind of all degrees do love it:
'Tis Cash each Man desires to have, and keep it,
He that does not, Quæ te dementia cepit,
May well be said of such, for't comes to pass,
Where Money's wanting every silly Ass
Insults o're you, his Tongue is there let loose,
Altho he scarce can say, Bo, to a Goose.
Money procures Respect, to every Fool,
He's Capp'd, and Cring'd, tho he look like an Owle.

78. *On Butter Searchers.*

IF th' Butter Searcher, do some Firkins find,
Not perfect Right, yet some times he'l be kind,
And pass 'em by, if th' Owners he do know,
And be assur'd they'l kindness to him show,
And presents make unto his Wife, or Self,
For tho no Money Bribes this Cunning Elfe,
Would be suppos'd from any to receive,
Yet he will take, what other things you'l give,
If any call these Bribes, he hath this shift,
Will tell you no, what is more free then Gift,

If you, Corn, Geefe, or Turkyes, will fend in,
He'l take 'em kindly, and will think't no Sin.

79. *On Farryers.*

IF you've an Horfe that's fick or Lame, wants Cure,
When e'er the Farryer comes, he'l you affure
That he can cure him, and will undertake
That he'l perform great Feats, for Moneys fake ;
He knows how many Bones, and Joynts, as plain,
And every finewe Artery, and Vein,
Are in your Horfe, and where and how they lye,
As if he'd Read upon Anotamy :
And yet for all his Skill, we often fee,
That he does clear miftake the Mallady,
Which being not by him right underftood,
He oft gives that, which doth more harm than good ;
And fo inftead of Curing of your Horfe,
He makes him every day, farr worfe and worfe,
Until at length, he turns up's heels and Dye,
And yet the Horfe-Leech you muft fatisfie
For his Medicaments, Labour and pains,
And fo your lofs, at length becomes his gains;
I've known a Noted Farryer fo Mifled,
He's faid an Horfe was ftrain'd, or Tifled,
And has hot Oyles unto the Horfe apply'd
For fome few dayes, until it was Elpi'd
The Horfe was Gravelled, and did break out
Above the Hoofe, which put it out of doubt,

He wonders then, he should so far mistake,
And sayes he now must other Measures take,
He Cuts the hoof, finds all within decay'd,
The Horse will lose his hoof, I am afraid,
Cryes he, then long time tampers with the same,
Till th' Horse is Ki l'd or at the best proves Lame,
And yet tho through this Fellows Ignorance,
To you befalls this dammage and Mischance,
He'l have the Confidence Money to ask,
Though he thus fondly have perform'd his task
But yet I think if he had his desert,
To pay for th' Horse in such case is his part.

80. *On the Horse Jockey.*

THe Cunning Jockye Feeds,and Graithes his horse
   In hopes that he thereby shall fill his purse,
With white and Yallow Ore, which will Revive
His drooping thoughts, when he finds he shall thrive :
Boyl'd Corn, with mash, and Balls, and other things
He gives his Horse, which he knows quickly brings
And plumps him up, makes him look fat and Fair,
And for a Market handsome viewly ware,
And tho he know in this, there's m███████
Yet he to get him off, doth use this Cheat,
I'ts Money that he wants, and her he'l have,
So Tricks will play, Money to get or save,
She is the dear prolubium of his Mind,
And to get her, he many wayes will find.

81. *On the power of Money in Eſtrangeing a Man from his Acquayntance.*

IF your Acquaintance which you once have known,
Was rich, and's now grown poor, you'l ſcarce him own
Eſpecially if you foreſee and know,
He comes to beg, or ſomething ask of you,
You'l not Remember then, that you before
Have ſeen him, walk Sir, trouble me no more;
O fie on Money, that ſhe ſhou'd thus make,
A Man his old Acquaintance to forſake.

82. *On Badgers.*

FRom Market unto Market the Poor Badger
Doth Ride and Run, and make himſelf a Cadger
Of Corn, from place to place, and takes great pains,
And all is but to get a little gains,
And if with proffit Money does but come,
He with Rejoycing then Returneth home,
Money revives his heart, if ſhe'l be found,
For her dear ſake he'l ſeek the Country Round:

... *a Gentlemans Shepheard.*

IF you have ſuch a ſtock and ſtore of Sheep,
That you a Shepheard are Enforeſt to keep,
Then over him you ought to take ſome care
For they oft times Knaviſh, and Roguiſh are;

Not

Not pleafed with their wage, more gains to make,
A fheep or Lamb, they now and then will take,
Then fhow their Skins, and by fome Dogs they'l fay
Chafed they were, and kild but Yefterday,
Or by Misfortune, fell into fome Ditch,
And fo were drown'd: Money doth them Bewitch,
To fteal the Muttons, their needs to fupply,
Then think t' excufe the matter with a Lye,
He that gives too much Credit, and believes
His Servants at all times, fhall make 'em Thieves.

84. On Inn-Keepers.

IF to an Inn you come, and freely call,
O then, the Mafters Company you fhall
Forthwith enjoy, there's nothing can withftand,
But he is folely Sir, at your Command,
The Hoftler is call'd in to take a Glafs,
The Mafter chargeth him before he pafs,
To take care of your Horfe, and rub him clean,
That not a bit of dirt be felt or feen,
Set him in the clofe ftall and fill his Rack,
And let him Eat until his Belly Crack,
Then feed and Water him in time, if you
Expect the Gentleman fhall kindnefs fhew,
Then you, and th' Hoft do fit and Bowze about,
And try which of you two does prove more ftout,
And when the one of you does Drowfie grow,
It's then high time, for you to call and know

To fee your Lodging-Chamber and the Bed,
Where you muft Reft and lye your Drowfie-head;
I'th' Morning you reioyce to meet again,
And fall afrefh into a merry Vein;
And when you're for your Journey, then comes in
The Land-Lords dram o'th' Bottle, he'l begin
Your health, wifh you an happy Journey home,
Seldome fuch Guefts unto his houfe do come:
That Money freely fpend and fill his Purfe,
For when the Niggard comes it is a Curfe,
He for a Single pot will call, and fit,
And fpend an hour at leaft in Drinking it,
Then out he walks to fee his Horfe i'th' Stable,
And then comes in, and bids 'em fpread the Table,
And let him have his Supper very Quick,
For he'l to Bed, he feels he's fomewhat fick,
Such Guefts the hoft had rather be without,
And when they're gone, he doth deride and flout;
So Money's certainly the only thing,
That Men to favour and Refpect doth bring
And he that wants it, is Efteem'd a flave,
And the Poor Man that cannot pay, a Knav

85. On Vintners.

THE Vintner, if you are a Conftaint Gueft
And Nobly fpend, you need not to requeft
The Choiceft Wine, for he will on his word,
Bring the beft in, his Cellar will afford,

And sit down by you, not go out of Sight,
Nor leave your Company by day nor Night,
So long as you will sit and Drink good Wine,
Tho it be ne'er so late he'l not repine,
Money comes finely in and that's the thing
Rubs off all carefull thoughts, and makes Men sing;
When you are weary grown, can Drink no more,
Your Gust, and Appetite for to restore,
Then Olives and Anchovies are brought in,
Which when you tast, afresh you do begin,
Place me Three or Four Bottles more in sight,
And them you Sipple off, then bid Good-Night,
But when the Miser doth come in and call
For gill, or Pint of the best Wine, you shall
The drawer cryes, have that that's very fine,
Canary, Rhenish, White, or Clarret Wine,
Let me a Gill of your best Sack then have,
You shall, you shall he Cryes, and then the Knave
Good and bad Wine doth mix, then up doth pass,
And pours some neatly out, into the Glass,
How Nitty, and how Raisie't looks cryes he,
This is good Wine Sir, if you'l Credit me,
The Miser Tasts, and Smacks it in his Mouth,
I doubt you've Cheated me, you Cunning Youth,
Upon my word Sir, 'tis the very best,
None such I'd draw, were't not at your Request,
Pray tast it then, he Sups, and Squirts it out,
Why Sir, what ails this Wine, you'l not find out

A

A ..... Glafs i'th' Town, this I dare fay,
.... Drinks it off, fo goes his way.
.. h Sufpect there's better Wine i'th' Houfe,
.. for th' Cuftom, that's not worth a Loufe,
.... do freely fpend, the beft Wine may
..., when thofe that do not, are faid nay.

86. On the Wine Marchants.

.. the Wine Marchants Cowper chance to light
.. Upon a peece of Wine, that's good and Right,
The Marchant faves't for him that payes the beft,
And fends it in to him, without Requeft,
That all the Town throughout, he may out brave,
That fuch a peece of Wine none of them have.

87. On Porters.

POrters at Tavern doors, or fome ftreet end,
  With Pokes, and Cords, do conftantly attend,
To wait a Turn, or on an Errand go,
Or goods and Luggage, carry to and fro,
And thus from day to day in Heat and Cold,
In weather wet and dry, this Courfe they hold,
Labour and any hardfhip they'l endure,
So they thereby can Money but enfure;
Money's the Pharmacotheon indeed,
That Cures Mens grief in greateft time of Need.

88. *On Hackney Coach-Men.*

THE Hackney Coach-Man, when he fees it Rain,
Is Pleas'd therear, tho others do Complain
For he's in hopes to have then a good Trade,
Whereby great ftore of Money will be made,
He values not, though he be wet to th' skin,
If he can get but ftore of Money in,
In wet and Cold he'l drive, tho Storms be great
And in hot Weather moile in duft and Sweat,
And in his Coach-Box, with great patience fits,
For Money runs betwixt him and his wits,
His mind is wholly fixt upon his Gains,
'Tis Money that does recompence his pains.

89. *On Foot Men, and Boyes.*

FOot Men and Boyes, behind a Coach do fit,
Oft times, when as their Mafters Ride in it,
They other whiles Run by their Mafters fide,
When they in Coaches, or on Horfe back Ride,
Sometimes they follow them, and Cloaks do carry
Sometimes at Doors Attendance give, and tarry
Afwell in darkeft Night, as in the day,
Till th' Mafters Pleafure is, to go away,
This Life they lead, they run, they go, they wait,
With patience take't becaufe it is their Fate,
From generous hands, they oft with Money meet,
Which bitter Toyle, and flavery, makes fweet,

There's

There's few but they will wait, and Run, and go,
If they be sure, they shall get Money so.

90. *On Hostlers.*

AN Hostler's lookt upon to be a Man,
That certainly will Cheat you if he can,
For tho you see your Horse with Corn well Fed,
And take great pains before you go to Bed,
To have your Horse's Rack well fill'd with Hay,
As soon as you are gone, he'l take't away,
And so your Horse all Night, stands without Meat,
Then the next Morn betime, that he no Cheat
May seem to be, he puts some in the Rack,
And sayes, Master your Horse no Meat did lack,
Your selfe did see, the Rack I did so fill,
That there is some remaining in it still,
And thus the Rogue his Credit would Retrieve,
Hopeing that what he sayes, you do believe;
If with your Corn, you Trust him to your Horse,
Then he, its like, will Cheat you worse and worse,
If you command him half a peck to give
Your Horse, then half as much he may Receive,
Or sometimes none at all, you must take Care,
Or otherwise your Horse will get ill Fair,
But this is unto such who strangers are,
Or pinching Slaves, for whom he doth not Care,
If you're a Constant Guest, and Nobly pay,
He'l neither Cheat you then of Corn nor Hay;

But

But will as honeft be in every cafe,
As if yourfelf were by him in the place,
For he's aflur'd, you will be very free,
And fo he deals with you in honeftie,
Immoderate Love of gains for his Reliefe,
Does tempt the Man, to make himfelf a Theif:
There's many have fo dearly Money bought,
That they themfelves have to the Gallows brought.

91. *On Common Carryers.*

THe drudging Carryers throughout the Year,
There loaden Horfes follow in the Rear,
In Winter time with many Storms they meet,
Early and late they go with cold wet Feet,
In Summer-time, they're all befmear'd with fweat,
Blinded almoft with Duft, their Feet fore beat,
And thus throughout the Year this courfe they Run,
In Winter Froze, in Summer Tann'd with th' Sun,
If for their pains you ask the Reafon why,
It is becaufe they Money get thereby,
Money's the Antidote 'gainft all diftrefs,
She comfort brings, unto the Comfortlefs, ·
That man no Trouble, pains, nor hardfhip feels,
Where Money furely follows him at th' heels.

92. *On Tapfters*

TApfters who th' Mafters Cellars Farm by great,
Will froth their Cans, and Pots, nick on, and cheat,
                                        Their

Their drink in Cans, Black Jacks, and pots will fill
Tankards, and little Muggs; for Cheat they will,
Both in their pinching meafure; and their Score,
As long as Money comes, they'l ne'er give o're,
Play all their Tricks, that they may hold her faft,
Till the Devil comes, and the Tapfter gets at laft.

93. *On Drapers and Mercers.*

IF you to th' Draper or a Mercer go,
With Cafh in hand, good penny-worths they'l fhowe,
Of Cloth, and Silkes, and Gold and Silver lace,
Buttons, and other things, for ufe and grace,
And if your Taylors Counfel here you have,
I'm fure by that, you'l neither gain nor fave,
If all at large be not Cut off, he'l fret,
For then poor Man he doth lefs Cabbage get;
If without Cafh, unto thefe Men you go,
And they your Credit, very well do know,
They'l fhow refpect, and tell you in a word
That as Cheap Penny-worths, they will afford,
As if you ready Money had, but when
Your Name is plac'd down in their Book, O then,
The fair tongu'd tradefman proves fo wondrous quick,
That you pay Ten per Centum for your Tick,
So if in three years time your fcore is pay'd,
He's a fufficient Gainer by his Trade.

94. *On Taylors.*

IF you to take up goods your Taylor trust,
   Then near the half of every thing he muft
Take for himfelf, as he doth take for you,
Thus to augment your Score, he helps to fcrew,
And if the Devil, do at his Elbow fit,
Yet he'l not fail to Cheat and fteal a bit,
So when the Taylor doth bring home your Clothes,
If you ne'er pay his Bill he cannot lofe.

95. *On Milliners.*

THE Milliner for ready Money's kind,   [find
   For Stockins,Ribbons,Gloves,Hoods,fcarfes,you'l
He'l ufe you well, and tho he do pretend,
He'd be as Kind becaufe you are his Friend,
Tho you don't pay, but upon Credit take,
But then be fure another price he'd make,
So truft him not, for Money always hath
More kindnefs found,then where there's greateft Faith.

96. *On Barbers.*

YOur Cringing Barber, will Powder and Comb
   Your new Bob Wigg, and to you bring it home,
Then puts it on your Head, and Curles does fet,
It fuits you well faith he, does finely fit,
'Tis Cheap Sir, of a Guinea, as e'er I made,
Since I firft Learnt, and underftood the Trade,
                                                    And

yet for Fifteen ſhillings paid in hand,
eady caſh this Wigg you may command,
en Sir your fine long Wigg muſt ſurely be
t down i'th' Barbers Book at Guinnies three,
When you for fifty Shillings payd on ſight,
The ſelf ſame Wigg, or elſe a Better might
Have put into your hands, finely ſet out,
With many thanks, and Congie too to boot,

97. *On Chyrurgions.*

THE Chyrurgion where he does Money find,
He often Viſits, and proves very kind,
Your wounds with ſuch great ſafety he will dreſs,
That he all Feavouriſh Symptoms will Repreſs,
And if your Wounds do chance to be enflam'd,
Or with ſome obtuſe Weapon you are Maim'd,
And bruiſed ſore he then will breath a Vein,
Remove black Yellow ſpots, and eaſe your pain,
But then for Money ſometimes he'l Retard
Keep back the Cure, that you will think its marr'd,
Then he will Laugh, and tell you that he could
Have Cur'd you ſooner, if ſo be he would,
But then he tells you, he muſt ſearch the Wound
To th' very Bottom, if you would be ſound,
And firm indeed, and have no after ſore,
And ſo become, worſe then you were before;
Theſe Men for Money too, can alſo Cure
The Flux, Pox, Aſthmaes, and the Calenture,

Coughs

Coughs, Rheumatisms, Costivenefs, and pains
In the fmall guts, or giddinefs i'th' Brains,
They many Cures can do for Moneys fake,
Which if't were wanting, they'd not undertake;
For when the Poor under their hands do lye,
Friend we can Cure you, prefently they'l cry,
But you muft look about, and Money bring,
To pay for and difcharge this and that thing,
So as the Poor Man doth for them provide,
Good or bad News to him, it doth Betide,
For to fay Truth, oft times for want of Coft,
Many poor Man's undone and meerly loft,
For where there Money lacks, it's very fure,
There will be no Attendance, care nor Cure.

98. *On Druggifts.*

DRuggifts found druggs nor Medicines will fend,
    But where their money's fure, tho you're their friend
For Ingenuity and Friendfhip too,
Altho for what is good, they Court and woo,
If Moneylefs, they go with empty pots,
When other thick Scull'd Idle filly fots
With Money can prevail, in a great huff,
To have the beft, whilest others take the ftuff
That's all decay'd, worm-eaten, old and Rotten,
For without Money, Friendfhip is forgotten,
And you muft wait their time, attend their call,
Perhaps get fome, perhaps get none at all,

If

If you get any, 'tis then with a flout,
And such old Stuff, you'd better be without
Then have it in your Shop, all will deny it,
And all your Customers you will lose by it:
So it is plain, there's none can drive a Trade,
Without good store of Money can be made,
Money does all things Master, all adore her,
Nought can withstand, she drives on all before her

99. On Shoomakers.

WHere the Shoomaker knows there's ready p..
He'l make choice ware for such, observe their
And for his stuff, together with his pains,
For ready Cash, he's pleas'd with Mod'rate gains
But where he knows, your pay's of longer date,
Then patiently you must his Leisure wait.
Then Rotten Neat, or Calf and Neat together,
With inner Soles put in, of base Horse Leather,
And such deceitful stuff, to you he'l Bring,
Yet have the Face to Brasen out the Thing,
The ware is firm and good upon his word,
Tells you, none such to others he'd afford,
All which is true, for they must better have,
You grope not out, the meaning of the Knave,
And then a price he sets (for 'tis his Trade)
Higher then on the choisest ware is made,
Thus they that Money lack, have th' hardest fate,
They're Cheated First, then pay Excessive Rate.

100. *On Watchmakers.*

YOur watchmakers, a neat good peece will fix
For four Pounds in hand, on Credit Six,
A Clock, and Weather-glafs, you too may have,
Which if you buy with ready pay you fave,
In each fix Pounds a Guinnie, if not more,
Such are the Fruits of Ticking on the Score,
When Tradefmen fell on Credit they take Care,
T' have Double Ufury paid 'em, for their ware.

101. *On Upholsters.*

IF the Upholfter to your Houfe do come,
To fet fome Beds up, or to Hang a Room,
If you pay down, the price you make him fet,
And bring him down as low, as you can get;
But if you Tick, that is a Curft difeafe,
For them he fets whatever rate he pleafe.

102 *On Jack of all-Trades.*

CAncs, Piftols, Knives, Guns, or what other Knack,
Or thing, in Jack of all-Trades fhop you lack,
If you are his Acquaintance he will fay,
Your Truft to him's as good as ready pay,
But this is fham, for where you go o'th' fcore,
You'l find you pay him a Third penny more,
Shew ready Coin, and then you bring him down
By Wrangling, from a Noble to a Crown.

103. On

103. On Sword-Cutlers.

THE chattering Sword-Cutler, will pretend,
He's such Respect, and is so much your Friend,
That you shall have the best, and choicest ware,
Pay or pay not, all's one he does not care,
But for all this, all Men may Understand,
That there no Friendship is, like pay in hand.

104. On Sadlers.

THE Sadler a fine Sadle, with good Bolsters,
Imbroider'd-house, good Stirrups, and fine Holsters
Brings to your Lodgings, tells you that 'tis Rich
Has cost him many hour, and carefull Stich,
I've layd out all my Moneys, dare you trust,
Say you, Yes Sir sayes he, I wish you durst,
Take so much Ware, as I dare Credit you,
You should have all I have, both Old and New,
Well what's the price say you, that I must give,
Sir just five Pounds, whether you take or leave,
O what this want of Money is with Men,
Money in hand, would fetch't, at Three pound-ten.

105. On Coach Makers.

A Painted Coach and harness fine and gay,
For Thirty Pounds you'l get, in ready pay,
But if they are brought in upon the score,
The price will then be Forty Pound or more:

O Money fie, great are the Cheats thou plays,
To Compafs thee, Men care not by what ways
They do proceed, and Value not a pinn
For Right or wrong, if Money comes but in,

106. On Brafiers, and Pewtherers.

THE Brafier and Pewtherer feldome give
Credit, but with Refpect they'l you receive
Into their fhops, will fhow what Wares you will,
London Pewther or double Metal fell,
At as low Rates, as poffibly they can,
For Money muft be had, fhe makes a Man;
Where Money's wanting each one will difpife
Tho you Jngenious be, and ne'er fo wife.

107. On Cabbinet makers.

THE Cabbinet Maker has Cabinets,
Tables and Drawers, Standards, Glaffes, fets
Of dreffing Boxes, Brufhes, and Jappan
Work of all Sorts; in every thing he can
Serve you as well, as any Man in Town;
At eafie Rates, if Money you pay down,
But when that wanting is, the Man looks fhy,
And matters not tho you fhou'd nothing buy,
Money is fixed in his Thoughts and heart,
And without her, he cannot freely part,
And leave his Goods, for if he's forc'd to Truft,
O then great and Exceffive gains he muft

Receive

Receive at length or elfe he will take home
His goods, Until a better Chapman come.

108. On Gold-Smiths.

THe Gold-Smyth when he fhews, and fells his plate,
Cannot with eafe Impofe, or put a Cheat
On you, for that is to be underftood,
Where it's Try'd by the Standard, and found good,
But when you come amongft his Rings to Gaze,
Diamonds, and Rubies, Emeralds, and Topaze,
Carbuncles, Hyacinths, and many more,
Which he will fhew amongft his Gliftring ftore,
Pearls Necklaces, Pendants, and Jewels too,
All which do make a great and glorious fhew,
To value thofe the Buyer wanteth skill,
So th' Gold-Smith fets the price down as he will;
If Money in his heart bear Rule; then he
Will prize them at a very high degree,
Or if he's pleas'd to take a Moderate gain,
As he will tell you, yet it's very plain,
Let th' price which you do pay be what it will,
If afterwards you're forceft to pawn or fell,
They'l fay they've gotten Water are all Soil'd,
So that the Sparkling Lufture of 'em's Spoil'd,
When as in Truth, they're not a penny worfe,
Then when you bought them firft, but O the Curfe
Of Money, whofe Delufions have the power
To make her Lovers right or wrong purfue her

The

The things for which you Twenty Pounds have given
Perhaps they'l have the Face to bid you Seaven,
Their Confcience fays, where Money does come in,
To Swear, diffemble, Lye, and Cheat's no Sin.

109. *On Grocers.*

THE Grocer, tho. he do not raife his price,
   Yet he'l put off his faulty Rotten Spice
Where you do Tick ; If ready Money comes,
Then you have Raifins, Plump and round as plumbes,
And if you take a parcel, he'l afford,
The Choyfeft Spice he hath, upon his word,
And he will pick and cull them out fo clean,
That not a Stone, or ftalk, 'mongft them is feen,
But if you Tick, you muft take what they'l give,
And have your Choyce, either to take or leave,
For you can not Expect, you may Command
Such ware, as thofe with Money in their hand.

110. *On the Tobacconift.*

WHere the Tobacconift good pay doth get,
   The choyceft Boxes up for thofe he'l fet,
But if you're flow in payment ; do not hit
His time, then any nafty trafh is fit
For you, cut ftalks mixt with decayed Stuff,
That's fit for nought, but grinding into fnuff,
If you complain and give't a bad Report,
He fends you word, 'tis very good o'th' Sort,

And

And th' beſt he had made ready up for ſale,
But come and clear of ſcores, then he'l not fail
To pick and Chooſe you out ſo good a ſort,
That when you come to Try't, you'l thank him for't,
Thus Money, Money, Runneth in his mind
Which you muſt pay if you'l true friendſhip find.

III. On Joyners and Carpenters.

JOyners and Carpenters a prey will make
Of you when they a peece of work do take,
If you in Timber-Meaſure have no skill,
Then they ſtrange ſtoryes unto you will tell,
Make you believe more Timber they muſt have
By far than ſuch a peece of work doth crave,
If they perceive you've Knowledge in the thing,
Then their Contriv'd deſign about to bring,
They tell you Nails and pins are in their task,
So they can not abate of what they ask,
If you're not willing ſuch a Summe to pay,
They tell you then, they'l work with you by day
If you agree but either way, O then,
They think themſelves for that time, happy Men,
For many Idle day-workes then you'l have,
Whether by day or Task, you'l nothing ſave,
For they're Reſolv'd good wages to bring in,
And tho unjuſtly got they think't no Sin,
Money's the Siren, Charmes their Eares and hearts,
Her to Acquire, they'l practice all their Arts.

1,2. *On Butchers.*

Butchers oft times their Flesh puff up and Blow,
That it may plumper and more viewly show,
By means whereof the Buyers they do Cheat,
And with their stinking Breath, do spoile the Meat,
Then when they've Lamb, or Veal, that's lean and silly,
Th' Kidneyes they'l stuff, and skewer up, then tell ye,
The Meat is fresh, and good, plump, fat, and fair,
But when you try't, you'l find it putrid ware,
They Meazell'd pork, and flesh dead by Mischance,
Or of some bad disease, will dare t'advance,
And lay upon there stalls, and sell't for good,
When they know well it is unwholsom Food,
And they should punisht be, for selling such,
But if they Money get, they care not much
Though they that se't, into diseases fall,
They do not care Money's their all in all.
And if you to their shop do send for Meat,
To have it fresh, you'l find they'l put a Cheat
On you, altho they'l promise fair and say,
You shall no more then other Buyers pay,
Yet three-pence, or a Groat a Joynt they'l have
More then the Market price, which you might save
If you th' Market sent, and wrangled there,
But you perhaps a Servant cannot spare;
Thus every Trade for greediness of gain,
Will Cheat and Lie, 'tis Evident and plain.

113. On

113. *On Sempstresses and Habberdashers.*

THE Sempstress, and the Habberdasher prate,
Make you believe, they sell at th' lowest Rate,
And say they do not set a doit down more
Then if you paid in hand, run not o'th' score,
For Beavers, Casters, Felts, Necks and Crevats,
Handkerchers, Ruffles, Caps, but these are Chats
And all meer Banter, Tradesmen cannot live,
Without Exacting, where they Credit give.

114. *On Scotch-Pedlars.*

THese Circumvoraneans, Scotch-cloth cry
Or Hollands, Muzlins, Cambricks, will ye buy,
Callicoes, Lawns, or any other ware,
If you'l buy nought then will you sell some Hair,
Thus at the doors and Windows they do call,
Several denials quiets not their Baul,
Into your house with Confidence they'l go,
Name all their Wares, and scarcely be said no,
From house to house, from Town to Town, they Run,
They'l spare no pains if Money can be won,
Either by Chaffer, or else otherwise,
So fair and tempting Money's in their eyes,
They'l seek and have her, if she may be found,
Traverse the Country, and whole Counties round
Country and Counties, did I say? We find,
To range whole Kingdoms, will not please their mind,
What

What Master Cleaveland, heretofore descry'd
May to these Pedlars fitly be apply'd,
Had Cain been Scot, God wou'd a chang'd his do.
Not made him Travel, but Confin'd him home.

115. *On Book-Sellers.*

THE Book-Seller, for ready Cash, will sell
   For as small profit, as another will,
But then you must take special Care and look,
You no new Title, have to an Old Book,
For they new Title-pages often paist,
Unto a Book, which purposely is plac'd,
Setting it forth to be th' Second Edition,
The third, or Fourth, with 'mendments and Addition,
But when you come, for to peruse and look,
You will not find one word in all the Book,
Put either in or out, or yet Amended,
For that's a thing which never was intended
By th' Authour, but when e'er a Book doth fail
This is their Trick, to quicken up the Sale,
But when a new Edition comes indeed,
From all the Old Books, which they have, with speed
The Title-Pages then, they often tear,
And new ones in their places fixed are
And have the Confidence to put to sale,
Such Books for new, they know are old and stale,
And so the Buyer, if he don't descry,
Will have a Cheat put on him purposely,

                        And

And when an Authours Books do bravely fell,
As thofe of th' whole duty of Man, do well,
And others, then to gain a Book a Fame
They'l fet it forth, under fuch Authours Name,
Prefixing an Epiftle to fuch Tract,
Declaring to the Reader matter of Fact,
How and by whom, the fame was brought to light,
And who hath had the view thereof and Sight,
How worthy the fame Book is of the prefs
And reafons why, it's publifht in fuch drefs,
With bantering ftuff, to make the Coppy fell,
Which pollicies they think, do wondrous well,
But thofe grand Book-Sellers, are much to Blame,
When a good Authour's dead, t'abufe his Name;
Such Tricks they play, and Act without Controll
For Moneys fake, there's fome would pawn their Soul,
If you, Vendible Books cull out, by fuch,
You may fuppofe, you cannot then lofe much,
But you're deceiv'd, for if you come to try
And put them off, you'l find them very fhie,
And Nice, they'l fay though at firft coming forth,
Thefe Books fold well, yet now they're little worth,
So Money to disburfe, they have no Mind,
'Caufe when to get it in they do not find,
But after much ado, you may contrive,
For Twenty pounds laid out to get in five,
And this they'l tell you meerly is to fhow
What favour and Refpect they have for you;

F.

If you'l Exchange for other Books fay they,
We can afford you then, fome better pay :
Ten Pounds in Truck, they will pretend is given,
When as the Books you get are fcarce worth Seven,
If to be Bookly given then be your fate,
You'd need to have a plentiful Eftate,
For when the Itch of buying Books grows ftrong,
Then you a prey to th' Book-Seller ere long
Become, he'l fend you Books, and truft fo much,
Until he find you fail for to keep touch,
Then for his Money he will call amain,
And if you pay but half, he gets good gain :
His Books are fo high priceft : but all or none,
That is the only ftring, he plays upon,
He'l take no Books again, in part, O Curfe,
He muft have ready Money in his Purfe,
And thus by him you're alwayes kept in Awe,
By conftant dunning, and threats of the Law,
When an Authour doth, to the Book-Seller bring
A Copy for the Prefs, altho the thing,
He knows will fell, yet he'l pretend and fay,
Paper is dear and Trading doth decay,
Money is fcarce, and Lycencing is dear,
So if he buy the Copy, he's in fear
To lofe by th' Bargain, yet at length he'l come
And condefcend to give you fome fmall fumme,
In part of which, a Parcel you muft have
Of Books, at his own price, and thus you flave
                                    Yourfelf,

Yourfelf, beating your Brains, and taking pains,
And this fame greedy Leech fucks up the gains,
He's fo in love with Money, that he'd ftarve
Authour, and Printer too, if he can ferve
But his own ends, and all the profit get,
He does not care how meanly they do fit.

116. On Printers.

THE Printer will for Money hazard fate,
  Print Scurrilous Pamphlets againft the ftate:
Or any dangerous Unlycenc'd thing,
Which may, Life and Eftate, in danger bring:
Such is the power of Money every where,
That Men regardlefs are of fhame and fear,
Nothing's too dear for Her to fet at ftake
That all this hurry in the World do's make.

117. On Higglers.

HIgglers with poultry, Eggs, and other Trade
  Do nod, and Ride all Night, are not affraid
Of weather, or bad way, or any harm,
Money againft all Fear's a powerful Charm,
The love of her runs in their Minds and heads,
She breaks their fleep, they reft not in their Beds,
But day and Night do Travel here and there,
Sometimes to fell, fometimes to get more Ware,
And thus continually they Ride and Rove
Money t'increafe, the only Mifs they Love,

She

She pays their Rent, fupplyes their needs they fee
And in their greateft Troubles, fets them free.

118. *On petty Chapmen.*

THE petty Chapmen, with Tobacco, Spice,
 Sope ftarch, and walnuts, Jndico, Blue, Rice,
Pepper and Ginger, Sugar White and Brown,
Brade, Thread, and Pins, they go from Town to Town,
Tape, Filletting, with many other Thing,
Which People want, from houfe to houfe they bring:
To Faires and Markets too, likewife they Rove,
Money to get, their ftocks for to Improve,
Money's the Mifs, for whom they fo much Itch,
Some her Obtaine, and by the Trade grow Rich.

119. *On Travelling petty Book-Sellers.*

THE petty Bibliopoll hath Hyftories,
 And fome fmall Books of feverall Miftories,
Primers, Pfalters, Bibles on his ftall,
Logiftorics and Books protreptical,
Such as he thinks are for the Peoples ufe
And his fmall Library doth then produce,
He them in Order viewly fets to th' Eye,
Hopeing they'l tempt fome lookers-on to buy,
He Money wants nought has fuch charms as fhe,
For her he'l part with his whole Library.

120. On

120. *On Linnen-Weavers.*

THe Linnen-weaver, houfe-wives yarn doth take,
   And they conclude how many yards t' will make,
Then fhe conceives there's warp enough, and Woof,
But fhe's deceiv'd when as it comes to th' proof,
The Cheating Knave, fome of her Clews does throw
Into his Hell-hole, then he lets her know,
That he, her Web cannot get out o'th' Loom,
For lack of yarn, fo fhe muft fend or come
With fome herfelf, this News makes her admire,
That he fhould fend, more Yarn for to require
He fayes the Yarn does tender prove and nought,
Elfe there had been no need, more to have brought,
When as indeed the good Wife he doth Cheat,
Money to get, by this his Roguifh Feat,
Money's the Saga which doth him Enchant,
He'l rather part with's honefty, then want
Her Company, who gets what he doth lack,
For hungry belly, and for Naked back.

121. *On Hard-Ware-Men.*

THE Hard-ware-Man at Markets feldome fails,
   With knives, and Siffers, hammers, Locks, and nails
And Smoothing-Boxes, *Buckles,* Steels and Awls,
And Jerfey-Combes are laid upon their ftalls,
With many other things that People ufe,
Which he lyes all in fight, for Men to chufe

Such

Such things as they do lack, and give him pay,
Money's the Miss, for whom the Man doth stay
And with great patience waites until she come,
Then he with Joy does take his Journey home,
And when this Lady he doth thither bring
He and his Family Choreuma's sing.

122. On Tanners.

TAnners unkindly heats do often use,
  Unto their Leather, and thereby abuse
Those that do wear the same, for it proves nought,
When after into Boots and Shooes it's wrought,
Then the Shoomaker's Rogued for the same,
When as in truth the Tanners are to blame,
Who too hot woozes use, or over Lime
Leather, and will not give it, its due time,
Then other whiles for utter Soles they Raise
Such poor thin Hides, by their unlawful ways,
Which they know well, for such use are not fit:
These crafts they use, more Money for to get
Then Lawful wayes can compass them, or bring
And thus we see Money's the only thing,
At which all Trades and Mysteries do look,
And are resolv'd to have't, by hook or Crook,

123. On Woollen-Weavers.

THe Woollen-weaver, sleight and thin will weave,
  That he some of the Clews of Yarn may save,
                                                    And

And keep himfelf, which th' Owners to him brought,
To have their Cloth made ftrong, and firmly wrought
But whether th' owners, keep it for their ufe,
Or fhall Expofe'tt to fale, they'l find th' abufe,
For when't comes to be worn, t'will fhrink full fore,
And every day, t'will Run up more and more,
And in great Lumps wear out great fhame to fee,
And all this through the Weavers Knavery,
Who not content with's honeft wage doth Cheat
For their was Yarne to make the Cloth compleat,
But then the Knave lefs Money would obtain,
If he gets nought but by his Lawfull gain;
So He's refolv'd he Money will enfure,
He cares not by what ways he her procure,
Money's the Soveraigne Emprefs of his heart,
For her with honefty and Truth he'l part.

124. On Hawking Pedlars.

SOme Hawking Pedlars carry on their Backs,
Others with loaden Horfes, and great packs,
Of hollands, cambricks, Lawns Scotch-cloth, and hoods,
Callico, Muzlins, Lace, and fuch like goods,
Gloves, skarfes, gowns, Silkes, and Mantos ready made,
Ribbons, and Necklaces, with fuch like Trade,
With which they Hawk, i'th' Country, here and there
At Faires and Markets too, to fell their ware,
Money's the only Lady they purfue,
If her they can but Catch, they never rue,

G

Nor

Nor of their pains and Labour do Repent,
Money does falve up all with great Content.

125. *On Glovers.*

GLovers with Leather, and Gloves ready made,
Markets attend to drive their petty Trade,
In heat and Cold, they keep their conftant Stand,
When Money comes to take her by the hand,
She's the Amicula of their Affe&ion,
Chears up their Spirits, and yeilds them Refe&ion.

126. *On Common Brewers.*

THe Common-Brewer where he gets good pay,
Beft Liquors unto fuch he fends away,
But thofe that drive him long, and take no care
To pay, he any Swillings fends in there.

127. *On the Ale-houfe Keeper.*

TThe Ale-houfe Keeper, if you'l freely pay,
And nobly call, he'l fit by you all day,
All other Company he will Negle&,
And you're the only Man fhall have refpe&,
'Tis on the Noble Minded Man he Tends,
That cares not what comes in nor what he fpends,
Such Company's the Solace of his heart,
He's then your Humble Servant, will not part,
Money's fo Charming that She makes him fhun
All other Guefts, and after you to Run,

There's

But if you far a Single pot but call,
He for fuch Company cares not at all,
So any Man without Offence may fay,
That Plurimi paffim fit *Pecunia.*

128. *On the Influence of Money upon Severall Sorts of Traders.*

CHeefe and Fifhmongers, and likewife Furryers,
Pawn takers, Leather Dreffers, and Curryers,
Iron and Wood-mongers, Salters, Salefmen,
Cole Merchants, Scriveners, Fletchers, Ratailmen,
Bottle-makers, Horners, and Trunck-makers,
Cole-meters, Bowyers, white and Brown-bread-bakers,
Tallow and Wax-Chandlers, Cutlers and Saylors,
Cooks, Watermen, Skynners, and Merchant Taylors,
Girdlers, Leather Sellers, Painters, Poulters,
Founders, Embroyderers, Marblers, and Coopers,
Armourers, Cane-Sellers, Spectacle Grinders,
Felt makers and Silk Throwers, and Refiners,
Oyl Men, perfumers, Glafs Men, and white Tawers,
Confectioners, with Staplers, and Cloth drawers,
Makers of Glafs, Tobacco Pipes, and Combes,
Whips, Inftruments of Mufick, and of Tombes

White

White-fmiths,and meal-men,and Block makers,Brokers
Strong-Water-ftillers, Coffee Men, and Smoakers,
Stone-Cutters, Lufterers, and Lynnen-Drapers,
With Callender Men, and Makers of Papers,
Wool Packers Stationers Lorainers Clarks,
Plafterers, Fruiterers, Black-Smyths, all fparks,
And Fellow Tradefmen, all thefe men do crave,
Money by all their Trades to get and fave,
Familyes cannot be kept, nor Rents well payd;
Unlefs good ftore of Money's got, by Trade,
'Tis fhe brings Comfort to the Tradefmans Mind,
For then he cares not which way blows the Wind.
Cloth workers, Carders, Spinners, Bleachers preffers,
Tuckers and Fullers, Dyers, and Cloth Dreffers,
With Tummers, and Winders, Shearmen and Teafers,
Weighers, and Mixers, Seperaters, Greafers,
Markers of Rugs, of Coverlets, and Ticking,
Manchefter Tape, and what the Men are quick in,
Laft makers, Mill-wrights, Cappers, greafy Knitters,
Shinglers,and Wheel-wrights, with Turners,and fitters,
Thefe Traders all, in the purfuit of gains,
Early and late do work, and take great pains,
Money procures them all things that they lack,
A d where fhe's wanting, all things go to wrack.

129. *On Apprentizes.*

POor prentices, th' fpace of Seven year,
Or longer time, their Mafters ferve with Fear,

Have

Have many taunts, crabb'd words, and scornfull looks
More strictly kept, then Schollars to their Books,
Are sometimes beat, Inhumanely Abus'd,
T would pitty one to have their Dog so us'd,
Some Lads on silly Errands are sent out,
For petty things, for which some do them flout,
Some clean the shooes, fetch coles,& door stones sweep
Dress Stables out, and Masters Horse do Keep.
Maney cold bitter stormy Winter day,
Poor Boyes behind the Shop board Trembling stay,
Fingers and hands, so swell'd and Numb'd with Cold,
They scarcely any thing can take or hold;
When hands and Feet are Cold, if they desire,
Yet without Leave they must not come to th' fire,
Their fingers blow, behind Backs stand and wait,
Whilest th' Masters warm themselves, sitting in state,
Some Boyes are almost starv'd, for want of Meat,
Or't's Slubber'd so, when't comes, they cannot Eat;
Drudges and perfect slaves some Lads are made,
Before they can be Masters of their Trade,
These hardships they endure with hopes to see
Their Term expire, and then they will be free,
May set up for themselves, and take their Ease,
Having no Angry Master then to please :
But then may Sell their Wares and Money take,
Having endur'd great slavery for her sake:
Then they're in hopes to get a Vertuous Wife,
Whose Company's the Comfort of Mans Life

G 3

Who

Who for the further Sollace of their state
Will Money bring for her associate,
Then all their former Slavery's quite forgot,
When as a Treble Bliss falls to their lot,
Freedome, a Vertuous Wife and Money store,
What would a man in this life Covet more.

130. On Citty Carr-Men and dray Men.

CAr-men and dray Men, sometimes have great lifts,
And when they drive, are put hard to their shifts,
Oft-times in Narrow Lanes there's such a throng,
They hazard sore their Lives to pass along,
They pull, they lift, they Curse, they Bawl and flight,
And sometimes fall to down right Blows and fight,
All Blood and dirt, with Hair all torn they've been
And hardly can be parted they're so keen,
All this they undertake, and more then this,
For th' Love of Money, their Admired Miss,
She charmes them so, they'l any Toyle endure,
In Leather Coats and Frocks, to make her sure,
What pains can be too great her to acquire,
Whom all the world doth follow and admire,
In whose society there's such delight,
That princes do for her fall out and Fight.

131. On Country Collyers.

POor Country Collyers, Money to obtain,
In Heat and Cold, fair weather, and in Rain,

Through

Through thick and thin, in Mire, afwell as duft,
Early and late their Horfes follow muft,
And many weary footftep every Week,
They're forc'd to undertake Chapmen to feek,
Elfe Madam Money will not thefe men own,
And then they know, no favour's to them fhown,
But if this Lady they have in their hand,
They're fure they then may any thing command,
Corn, Bread, or Flower, Eggs, Butter, Flefh, or Fifh,
Or what elfe they for Back or Belly wifh,
Money's Queen Regent of the heart, all will
On her Attend, her pleafure to fulfill.

132. On Pavers.

THe paver when he works by Yard or Great,
He'l make his Tools and hands go till he Sweat,
As faft he'l pitch the Stones, and them will pave,
As Servers can the fame unto him heave,
Great pains he'l take to pave much on a day,
For then he know more Money's due for pay,
For Greedinefs of Money, thus he'l Cheat,
And take no pains firmly his work to beat,
But cover o're with Sand to make't appear
Firm to the Eye, when within halfe a Year,
It all breaks up, then all the Labour's Loft,
And th' Owner then is put to double Coft:
For if at firft the Stones he firmly fet,
Covers them well, and has them firmly beat,

Till

Till every Chinck is close fill'd up with sand
And no Stone higher then another stand,
But also Firmly beat, and close and plain,
That it will bear a Loaden Cart, or wayne,
And never Shrink, that is firm work indeed,
But Ah Sir then, he cannot make such speed,
Nor gits such wage, as he desiers to have,
For store of Cash, you've leave to call him Knave,
Money's the false Trivenesica we see,
Enchants Men to betray their Honesty,
Credit, good Name, and all that is most dear,
If she upon the Stage, do but Appear.

133. *On Fisher-Men.*

POor Fisher-men, to wait their time and Tide,
   In Sorry Cabbins near the water-side,
On straw, or Rushes, Poorly lie and Tumble,
And at their Fare, and Hardship never Grumble,
But draw their Nets and Lines, in Rain and Cold,
And are full glad when they do Fish behold,
And those poor men that Venture out to Sea,
When Stormes Arise, sometimes are cast away,
And so instead in Catching Fish for gain,
Themselves are Catcht by death, Entomb'd i'th' Main.
The hopes Men have, they Money shall command,
Makes them Adventure both by Sea, and Land,
Comfort she brings in time of greatest Need,
Men in their greatest Trouble she hath freed,

What Toyl or hazzard can be thought too much,
For Money then whole Company is such.

134. *On Brickmakers.*

THe poor Brick-makers in cold Winter weather,
Their Clay turn over, and do cast together,
In Summer time from Morn till Night, all Day,
With their bare hands, they work and mould their Clay;
In Flooring, Dressing, Drying and making fit,
They take great pains, ere th' Bricks in Kill are set,
They pile them close, and dawbe them round about,
Least when they 're fire d, it any where break out,
After this Toyl, then Money comes to please,
Their *Acopum Catholicum* of Ease.
Money their Toyl requites, gets Clothes and Food,
Makes those are Sad, be in a Merry mood.

135. *On Carters,* Wain-men *or* Waggoners.

CArters, Wainmen, and Waggoners for hire,
In Summers heat, and Winters Cold and Mire,
Be th' weather good or bad, they keep their Stage,
Because they know, it brings in constant wage,
Much Toyl they have, and many dangers run,
Money without great pains will not be won,
For he that Moneys company doth crave,
Besides great Care he must himself enslave,
Till he prevail to have her at his will,
With her assistance then he may fulfil.

what

What he defires, great Hills may level plain
Or in low Valleys raife great Hills again,
He any thing may to his Humour bring;
He that has Money can do every thing.

136. *On Glaſs Men, that Travel in the Country.*

THe Glaſs Man bears about upon his Back,
Glaſſes and drinking Pots, both White and Black,
He 'ſcapes ſome dangers, ſome he cannot paſs,
But now and then, he breaks a Pot, or Glaſs,
And yet he Travels on, hoping to have   .
A better Price, for thoſe he whole doth ſave,
Money he doth purſue, from Place to Place,
All hazards he breaks through, to ſee her Face.
Whatſoe'er Miſchances or Misfortunes fail,
If he get her, She makes Amends for all,
No danger's great, no pains too much can be,
To compaſs ſuch a Ladies Company.

137. *On Bowle Sellers.*

SEllers of Bowls, Chirns, Pales, and other Ware,
With them do ride about, from Fair to Fair,
Chapmen to meet, that ready Money bring,   .
Then they will ſmoak, bouz off their Potts and ſing,
When th' Market's bad, they're in a ſullen frame,
So dull that none wou'd think they are the ſame.
Money's the ſprightly Miſs, the Dainty Dame
That Cheareth up, both Young, Old, Blind and Lame.
138, On

138. *On Coopers in the Country.*

TH' Cooper, with Hoops & Tools does march about
  To find out work walks many a weary Foot,
Ween with a Jobb he meets and Money's got
He does rejoyce at his Aufpicious Lot.
When tyr'd with Work, and travelling all day,
Money makes him at Night fing Care away.

139. *On Travelling Potters.*

POtters to Markets with their brittle Ware,
  Poffeft with Fear, do March, and full of Care,
Leaft they againft fome Gate, or Style do run,
Or fall and break their ware, they're half undone,
Yet Madam Money, has them at her Call,
For th' Love they bear to her, they'l venture all,
The hopes they have, of her to be poffeft,
Difpels their Fear, at home they will not reft,
But out they'l go Money to feek and find,
The Supream Paralefis of their Mind.

140. *On Oatmeal Sellers.*

THe Venditors of Oatmeal round and fmall,
  Do diligently wait on Moneyes Call,
And when fhe doth appear, then at her pleafure,
This Oatmeal is deliver'd out by meafure,
As long as any in their Skeps remain:
For fhe the Sellers, can fet up again.

If

If Money they receive they do not care,
They for her sake will part with all their Ware,
Money's more worth. then the best Merchandize,
She's the dear Paramour in all mens Eyes.

141. *On Sellers of Roots in Markets.*

Sellers of Roots, who Markets do attend
Potatoes, and fine Cabbages to vend,
Turneps and Carrots, and an hundred more,
Of which their Gardens yeild abundant store,
With these they wait, and with great patience stay,
Till Money comes, and has them all away,
'Tis she they come to meet, and those that have
A mind to Roots must her assistance crave,
If she comes not, they get nor great nor small,
But if she comes, they may command them all,
When she appears, none can her Power withstand,
Where e'er she goes, all yeild to her demand,
Unles't be Death, he'l not her Charmes obey,
For when he comes, he will not be said Nay.

142. *On Sellers of Bread or Cakes in Markets.*

THose which with Bread, or Cakes in Markets sit,
Or round the Country, bear or carry it,
Though Bread's the Staffe of Life, yet they will part
With it, for Moneys sake, with all their heart,
Faith, Hope, and Charity, great Graces be,
And Charity the greatest of the three,

What

What Name and Place, does Money then deſerve,
Saves Life, when Charity would let you ſtarve.

143. *On Country Rope-Makers.*

THe Roper with his Ropes, of Hemp, or Hair,
Horſe-pannels, Wantyes, Cords and ſuch like ware,
Sackweb, with Halters, Hair Cloth too, he ſhows,
Cart-Ropes, and Hopples, for Horſes and Cows,
Theſe things for Money, he doth ready make,
Has them from Place to Place, Money to take,
For he to compaſs Her, no Place will miſs;
For She's *Solamen* in Miſeries.

144. *On Fiſh-Drivers*

DRivers of Fiſh, do unto Markets bring,
Cod, Scate, and Turbut, Haddocks, Trout and Ling,
Conger, and Whitings, Killing, and Mackrel,
With Lobſters, Cockles, and fine Crabs to ſell,
Salmons, and Scurfes, with Smelts, and Salmon Cocks,
Catcht in the Nets in Kiddels, or Fiſh Locks,
Winter and Summer, travel Night and Day,
Sometimes in good, ſometimes in dirty way,
And in great Storms, they're ſometimes almoſt loſt,
Thus for a Livelyhood, poor Men are Toſt,
When they to th' Market come and Fiſh ſet down,
They go their wayes, and ſtay ſome time i'th' Town
Return no more till latter end o'th' Day,
And then they know, thoſe People will not ſtay
Th:

That have far Home, and fo the Price they fet,
Upon their Fifh, they are in hopes to get,
Becaufe to wrangle, Buyers cannot ftand,
Rather than ftay will pay what they demand,
Thus every Trade does exercife his wit,
And all their Cunning Tricks Money to get
Her to acquire a Man his Life oft ventures,
And for her fake his Wit will fet oth' Tenters.

145. On Sievers and Basket Makers.

Sievers and Basket makers with made Wares,
As Baskets, Voyders, Sieves, and Wanded Chaires,
Fine Rangers, Searcers, Tiffanyes and Boulters,
Courfe and fine Scuttles, Panyers for Poulters
And fuch like things, with many other more,
Which they have alwayes ready made in ftore,
From Fair to Fair they Ride, and Markets ply,
Money to get, all Places they do try;
Money's the Mifs for whom they work and ftrive,
Them and their Familyes fhe keeps alive.

146. On Country Salters.

THe Common Salters all the Summer long,
To ferve the Country with their Salt are throng,
They Travel Day and Night, no time refrain,
Their Horfes graife in any Street, or Lane,
Their Salt to fave from Rain, with Skins they hide,
And nod and fleep as they on Horfe-back Ride,

Oft

Oft are they weary, and moft fadly wet
And yet well pleas'd if Money they can get,
Money's fo precious, Men no dangers fhun,
But will for her through Fire and Water Run,

147. On Tinkers and Bowle-Sewers

TInckers and Bowl-Sewers oft Ragged are,
So to get Money themfelves to repair,
When any Job of Work falls in their hand,
Three times as much for it they will demand
As they deferve to have: you muft Agree
Before the Work's begun, if you'd be free
From noife and Clamour, elfe the Rogues will fweat
And not give o're, till money does appear,
She Charmes them into filence, makes them ftill,
She Clothes their Backs, and does their Bellies fill.

148. On Thatchers.

THe Thatcher all day on a Ladder ftands,
The Thatch layes on and faftens with his hands,
His Work doth Cut, and Smooth, make trim and neat,
The Eves cut ftraight, and Ridges makes Compleat,
When throng he's pleas'd, for Money then is got,
Which makes his Spit to wag, and boiles his Pot,
She makes him work all day with great delight,
No Care or woe does break his fleep at Night.
Great Winds great mifchief unto fome do bring,
Yet they to him are clear another thing,

He

He laughs when Winds are great, for he doth know
It's an ill Wind, that none doth profit blow.

149. *On Chimney--Sweepers.*

THe Chimney Sweeper thinks it no disgrace,
For Money's sake, to have his hands and face
Besmeer'd with Soot and Nasty to the sight,
And tho he's Black all o're, he cryes all White,
His filthy loathsom Cleathes and noysome smell,
And Soot in's Eyes, he can endure full weil,
If Money comes but in, he then is Jolly,
And round about doth Trudge with's Polls and Holly;
And into any smutty hole will creep,
And Nasty stuff upon himself will sweep,
O Money Money, for thy Charming sake
Men any drudgery will undertake,
Think no Imploy disgraceful, or unfit,
So they can Money but acquire by it.

150. *On Kennell Rakers, and Ragg Gatherers.*

THe Kennel-Raker with his old scratch't Broom,
Backwards&forwards sweep where he doth come
And in those Places where he Sweeps, doth mind
If Horse-Shooe-Nails, or Iron he can find,
Or any thing, he thinks will Money make,
Which he with Joyful mind doth quickly take,
And into's old Hat Crown the same doth fling,
Which for that purpose, he about doth bring,

And

And thus from Street to Street, he trots about,
To seek his petty Merchandizes out,
Which to his Chapmen he does bear a way,
Who for the same afford him ready pay,
Then he with Joy to's Trade returns again,
For Money's sake, no drudg'ry he'l refrain,
Then they that seek about for Clouts and Raggs
And in By-places rake, that they the Bags
And Pokes, they for that purpose bring may fill,
And get a Stock up, for the Paper-Mill,
Where they get Money, which doth joy their heart,
And all their pains, they take then in good part,
For Money will get any thing they lack,
Both for their hungry Belly, and nak'd Back,
Men wet and dry, and heat and cold endure,
Take any pains to make some Money sure.

151. *On the Jakes-Farmer, or Gold-finder.*

THe Stinking Gold-Finder with his white Rod,
In Common, or in Private Jakes will prod,
And take the Depth, and Latitude thereof,
Endure the Loathsomness and every Scoff,
And scornful Flout, his stinking Trade affords,
And with his hands bare, rake in filthy ——
Abide the smell without offence to's Nose,
With Patience look upon his —— Cloaths,
I'th' Tubs and Buckets grope with willing Mind,
And try if he can Gold and Money find,

O who would think Lady *Pecunia* had
Such power, t'inveagle Men to be fo mad,
To follow Nafty Trades and ne'er complain,
If they this dainty Mifs, can but obtain,

152. *On Cow-herds.*

THE harmelefs Cow-herd trots and runs about,
    Both gathers in the Cows and drives them out,
For fome fmall Salary, the Poor Man waits,
Money though little, helps him in his ftraits
Money where e'er fhe comes, doth kindnefs fhow,
Comfort affords, pays all, or part Men owe,
Prevailes with thofe, that fierce and Cruel are,
Where fhe appeares, they further time will fpare.

153. *On Common Swine-herds.*

THE Common Swine-herds courfe, is every Morn,
    To go about the Town, and wind his horn,
Then People let their Hoggs go out at large,
And th' Swine-herd takes them all into his charge,
And into th' Fields he drives them day by day,
And there attends on them, the time they ftay,
And when fome fignes of Rain or ftormes appear,
Unto fome ditch or Hedge, he then draws near,
And under Banks does fculke, till Night does come,
Then's Army he drawns up, and Marches home,
And thus poor man, he fpends his Slavifh life,
Some Money to procure, for him and's Wife,

And

And Family, and tho it be but small,
He gets, it's better far, than none at all;
A little Money brings him some Relief,
But none at all, affords him nought but grief:
So when his Fair is mean, he ne'er complains,
But shapes his Mind according to his Means,

154. *On the Common daily Cryes,* *in and about London.*

WE dayly cryes about the streets may hear,
According to the Seafon of the year,
Some Welflet Oysters call, others do cry
Fine Shelsey Cockles, or White Muscles buy,
Great Mackrel, five a Groat some Cry about,
Dainty fresh Salmon, does another shout,
Buy my fine dish of dainty Eels cryes one,
Some soles, and flownders, in another tone,
Butter and Eggs some Cry, some Hampshire honey,
Others do call for Brass, or broken Money,
Have ye any old Suits, or Coats, or Hats,
Another sayes come buy my dainty Sprats,
Box, or Horn, Combes of Ivory, or Sissers,
Tobacco-Boxes, Knives, Rasors, or Twissers,
Who buyes my bak'd Oxe-Cheek, here in my pot,
Plump, fresh and fat, well Stew'd, and piping hot,
Dy'd Lin for Aprons, Vinegar some Cryes,
Some hot Bak'd Wardens, others, puddin pies,

Buy,

Buy a Jack-Line, or an Hair-Line cryes some,
New Books, New Books, then doth another come,
French Beans and Parsley, some cry, if ye mind,
And others, have ye any Knives to Grind,
Some Ropes of Onyons Cry, about the Town,
Some Pepins, and Pearmains, up Street and down,
Hot Codlins hot, the best that ere you see,
Who buyes these dainty hot Codlins of me,
Turneps, and *Sandwich* Carrots, one Man calls,
Green Hastings, in my Cart, another bawls,
Come buy a Steel, or a Tinder-Box, cryes some,
Old Boots or Shooes, sayes one, come buy my Broom,
Maids ha' ye any Kitchin-Stuff, I pray,
Buy long Thread Laces, does another say,
New Almanacks some cry, at th' times o'th' year,
Then others, singing Ballads, you may hear,
Some carry Painted-Clothes, on little Poles,
By which it's known, that such Men do catch Moles,
Others in Clothes will Painted Rats have made,
Which notifies, Rat Catching is their Trade,
Have ye any work for a Cooper here,
Old Brass to mend, then Tinckles one i'th' Rear,
Some Nettle-Cheeses cry, and some New Milk,
Others Sattin, and Velvet, or old Silk,
Then Ends of Gold or Silver, cryes a Lass,
Another Curds and Cream, as She does pass,
With traps, for Rats and Mise, do some appear,
Two hundred a penny, Card-matches here.

Ripe

Ripe Cherries ripe, come buy my Early Cherrys,
Who buys my Currans or large ripe Goose-berries,
A Rubbing Bruſh, a Bottle Bruſh, or Grater,
Fine Sparrow-graſs, then cryes another Creature,
Here's dainty Cowcumbers, who buyes to Pickle,
Another then, with Colly-flowers does ſtickle,
Ripe Raſs-berries, about, does ſome then ſing,
Fine young Strawberries does another bring,
Freſh Nettle-tops, or Elder-buds, come buy,
Then Water-creſſes, and Brooklime, they cry,
Any old Iron here to ſell cryes one,
And ſome Maids, ha ye any Marrow Bone,
Ripe Muske Mellons, or Apricocks, ſome Cry,
Fine Civil Oranges, or Lemmons Buy,
Old Chaires to mend, then Cryes a Ragged Fellow,
Come buy a Door Matt, does another bellow,
Buy a Cock or a Gelding, does one come,
Come buy my dainty Singing Bird, ſayes ſome,
Some dainty fine Holly and Ivy ſayes,
Then Curious fine Roſemary and Bayes,
Some Pens and Ink, would ſell to all they meet,
And others Small Coal Cry, about the Street,
Pitty th' poor Priſoners, ſome with Baskets go,
And others Cry, come ſee my rara Show,
Anon a poor Wretch comes Crying behind,
With Dog and Bell pray pitty the poor Blind,
Who buyes theſe Figgs and Raiſins new of mine
Come buy my Bowl of Wheat, fine Oatcakes, fine,

Hot

Hot Mutton Pyes, cryes one along the Streets,
Who buyes my Mutton Pyes fresh hot and sweet,
Buy Marking stone, one Cryes, with's smutty face,
Another sayes, come buy my fine Bone-Lace,
Buy a Cloth or Thrum Map, you Maids and Lasses,
Another Cryes, who buyes my drinking Glasses,
A Lattice for a Window, who will Buy
Great Faggots, five for Six-pence does some cry,
Have ye any old Glass for to renew,
Some cry Bellows to mend, or Bowles to sew;
Some Silk or Ferrit Ribbon, for shooe strings,
With London pins, and Tape and other things,
Have y'any Corns, upon your Feet, or Toes,
Buy a Fox Tail, or Whiske, another goes,
Some walk about, and old Silk-stockens Cry,
Some ask if Socks, or Quilted Caps you'l buy
And thus they Trot about and Bawl each day,
For th' Love they bear Lady *Pecunia*,
For her they'l sit up late, and Early Rise,
She does appear so Glorious in their Eyes,
Think all pains well bestow'd, nothing too much,
Their Zealous dotage to this Idol's such,
Money's the only she, all Men admire,
Both Poor and Rich, this Lady do desire,
And those that her do want, they are forlorn,
If she's not there, they're every Fellows Scorn,
We may conclude, when we've said what we can,
'Tis Money at all times, does make a Man.

155. *On Gripeing, and Oppressing Mortgagees.*

SOme Mortgagee, will at Advantage lye,
Upon the Rigour, of 's Security
He will infift, on Nicetyes will ftand,
He'l neither purchas all, nor part o'th' Land
He has Engag'd, nor will he let you reft,
But he with Threats, and Suits, will you moleft,
So neither fell the Land, nor Let, you can,
To th' beft Advantage, unto any Man :
By means whereof, he knows that he muft Seize,
Further he'l not Account, then he receives,
So he'l difpofe, and let at eafie Rate,
And fo will worm you out of your Eftate,
For he'l his purpofes fo bring about,
You'l never live, to fee the Mortgage out;
So by this Crafty means, he'l you compel
For prefent Maintenance, your Land to fell,
Then his own Terms he'l make, for him or's Friend,
Having now gain'd the point, he did intend :
If he be told his doings are unjuft,
To look for's own, he fayes he will, and muft,
The Law allows all he has done, he'l fay,
But Summum Jus eft Summa Jnjuria ;
And tho at prefent, it troubles not his Mind,
Yet afterwards, he'l wifh he'd been more kind,
When he on's death Bed lyes, he'l figh and grone,
No Mercy can Expect, that none has Shown,

His

His Confcience then t' accufe him, will begin,
Tell him Oppreffion is a Crying Sin,
And then he'l cry, wu'd he'd more favour fhown,
And wifh that he, the Land had never known;
The gains he's got, by the poor Debtors crofs,
He finds will now be his Eternal Lofs.
Money nor Lands, no Comfort, now do bring,
A good Confcience, is the fole Soveraigne thing;
He now with heavy groans, repents his Evil,
When he's afraid, he's going to the Devil:
Who at his Death will Mercy beg and crave,
Muft in his Life time Mercy fhew, and have.

156. On Berge Men or Loyter Men.

BErgers and Loyter-Men do Row and Bawl,
  By Night and Day, their Boats they pull and hawl
Many cold blaft, and bitter Storm they bide,
Be't fair or Foul, they will not lofe their Tide:
But out they'l go, no Weather them will ftay,
What is't that poor Men will not do for pay;
Money's the Crown of all their hopes, the prize
At which they aim, precious in all Mens Eyes,
Th' Apotheca of all Terreftrial good,
She brings to all both Clothes and Drink and Food.

157. On Intelligencers or News-Mongers.

THe News-Mongers themfelves Infinuate
  Into their favour, who çan tell the ftate
                                          And

And Face of Things, how they are mannag'd here,
And how transacted and defign'd elfewhere ;
To their Amanuenfes they Indite,
Who take the Heads, and feveral Letters write
Of News at large, then to the Country fend 'em,
And to th' Imployers there, do recommend 'em :
Thus Poft by Poft, they let them underftand
Th' Intreagues a foot, afwel by Sea as Land,
Money for this, they quarterly receive
From their Imployers, thus they bravely Live:
Then to th' Imployers Houfes Men repair,
And Money fpend, to read News-Letters there ;
Thus both News-mongers, and Imployers gain
Money on this account, or it is plain,
No News at home, from Foraign States, or *France*,
We fhou'd receive,but reft in Ignorance,
Money does pry into the fecret Things
Of privy Councils, and Gabals of Kings,
She Fairy like, unfeen creeps here and there,
Difcovers Plots tho whifper'd in the Ear,
And when the Stroke is ready for to fall,
She fhews the Clan, and difappoints them all:
Her Charms are fuch that none can them gainfay
She'l make a Man, his Bofom Friend betray.

158. *On Ferry Men.*

THe Ferry Men that Paffage Boats do keep,
Attend all Day, i'th' Night broke of their fleep

To wait on those, who that way do resort,
Them and their goods o're Rivers to Transport:
This Toyle and pains they take for Money's sake,
Ne'er grudge thereat, nor no Complaints do make,
For such like Men do think, that Money is
Th' Royal diploma, of all Earthly Bliss.

159. On Water-Men, or Wherry-Men.

THE Wherry-Men do wait at River's staires,
    And lanes near Water sides, expecting fairs,
When any come they think do want a Boat,
They run, hold out their hand, set up their Note,
Sculler and Oares they Cry, and stop your way,
Till th' Signe you give, they will not be said Nay,
And when a Jolly Company they get,
They'l cast their Coats, and Rowe until they sweat
And day by day, this Course they do attend,
For Madam Money's sake, their Chiefest Friend,
'Tis she on whom they solely do Rely
Them in their great distresses to Supply:
When her they have, of nought they stand in fear,
For nothing they can want, when Money's there,
Money's the Idol, that each Man Adores,
And her Assistance all the World Implores.

160. On Common Strumpets.

THE Lewd debauched Mercenary Miss
    For Money's sake, will any Fellow Kiss,

For

For fhe in that by far takes more delight
Than in the Luftful Carnal Appetite,
'Tis Money not the Man fhe doth adore,
Money's the Caufe fhe turns a Common whore
And proftitutes herfelf at any time,
Brute-like, and has no fence of any crime.

161. The Conclusion.

NOw Mufe farewel, for both to Age and Youth,
Thou haft difcover'd here, many a Truth,
Andtho in generall Termes, thou haft fet forth
The fame, yet there are fome of greater worth,
And Vertue, that above Temptation are,
Whom neither Gold nor Money can Enfnare,
A dirty, or unfaithful thing to Act,
Or their Allegiance fuffer to be Craft,
And fo no General Rule there is, but hath
An Exception, as the Old Proverb faith.
But thou haft fairly thrown each one their Lot,
Some thou perhaps has pleafed, and fome not,
For fome will Laugh, fome fret, and fome deride,
At that which here, to them thou haft difcry'd,
But in this Cafe, thou fafely mayft Conclude,
That none e'er yet could pleafe the Multitude,

162. The Epilogue.

AS I begun, fo I'll Conclude, and fay,
That Pecuniae Obediunt Omnia.

Mr Richard Hustler His Book
February ye 14 ~ 1700 ~

Richard Hustler

his Book

1698

Richard

Richard

Richard Hustler

Perfect Table of the Titles of the severall
Subjects Treated upon in this *POEM*.